the food and cooking of
Indonesia
& the Philippines

traditions • ingredients • tastes • techniques • 80 classic recipes

the food and cooking of
Indonesia
& the Philippines

Ghillie Başan & Vilma Laus
photography by Martin Brigdale

aquamarine

For my parents, a big thank you from Vilma and me
Kain na tayo!

This edition is published by Aquamarine,
an imprint of Anness Publishing Ltd,
Hermes House,
88–89 Blackfriars Road,
London SE1 8HA;
tel. 020 7401 2077;
fax 020 7633 9499

www.aquamarinebooks.com;
www.annesspublishing.com

If you like the images in this book and would
like to investigate using them for publishing,
promotions or advertising, please visit our
website www.practicalpictures.com for
more information.

UK agent: The Manning Partnership Ltd;
tel. 01225 478444; fax 01225 478440;
sales@manning-partnership.co.uk

UK distributor: Grantham Book Services Ltd;
tel. 01476 541080; fax 01476 541061;
orders@gbs.tbs-ltd.co.uk

North American agent/distributor:
National Book Network; tel. 301 459 3366;
fax 301 429 5746; www.nbnbooks.com

Australian agent/distributor:
Pan Macmillan Australia;
tel. 1300 135 113; fax 1300 135 103;
customer.service@macmillan.com.au

New Zealand agent/distributor:
David Bateman Ltd; tel. (09) 415 7664;
fax (09) 415 8892

ETHICAL TRADING POLICY

At Anness Publishing we believe that business
should be conducted in an ethical and
ecologically sustainable way, with respect for
the environment and a proper regard to the
replacement of the natural resources we employ.

As a publisher, we use a lot of wood pulp to
make high-quality paper for printing, and that
wood commonly comes from spruce trees.
We are therefore currently growing more than
500,000 trees in two Scottish forest plantations
near Aberdeen – Berrymoss (130 hectares/
320 acres) and West Touxhill (125 hectares/
305 acres). The forests we manage contain
twice the number of trees employed each year
in paper-making for our books.

Because of this ongoing ecological investment
programme, you, as our customer, can have the
pleasure and reassurance of knowing that a tree
is being cultivated on your behalf to naturally
replace the materials used to make the book
you are holding.

Our forestry programme is run in accordance with
the UK Woodland Assurance Scheme (UKWAS)
and will be certified by the internationally
recognized Forest Stewardship Council (FSC).
The FSC is a non-government organization
dedicated to promoting responsible management
of the world's forests. Certification ensures forests
are managed in an environmentally sustainable
and socially responsible basis. For further
information about this scheme, go to
www.annesspublishing.com/trees

NOTES

Bracketed terms are intended for
American readers.

For all recipes, quantities are given in both
metric and imperial measures and, where
appropriate, in standard cups and spoons.
Follow one set, but not a mixture, because they
are not interchangeable.

Standard spoon and cup measures are level.
1 tsp = 5ml, 1 tbsp = 15ml, 1 cup = 250ml/8fl oz.

Australian standard tablespoons are 20ml.
Australian readers should use 3 tsp in place of
1 tbsp for measuring small quantities of
gelatine, flour, salt, etc.

American pints are 16fl oz/2 cups. American
readers should use 20fl oz/2.5 cups in place
of 1 pint when measuring liquids.

Electric oven temperatures in this book are for
conventional ovens. When using a fan oven, the
temperature will probably need to be reduced
by about 10–20°C/20–40°F. Since ovens vary,
you should check with your manufacturer's
instruction book for guidance.

The nutritional analysis given for each recipe is
calculated per portion (i.e. serving or item),
unless otherwise stated. If the recipe gives a
range, such as Serves 4–6, then the nutritional
analysis will be for the smaller portion size, i.e.
6 servings. Measurements for sodium do not
include salt added to taste.

Medium (US large) eggs are used unless
otherwise stated.

Contents

Introduction

Indonesia and the Philippines provide a diverse culinary experience as a result of both their histories and their geographical locations. Situated in the middle of the ancient trade routes, Indonesia has a long history of colonial intervention, a factor that has influenced the cuisine, enriching it with spices and cooking techniques from India, Persia and China. The food of the Philippines, on the other hand, has been principally influenced by the Chinese and the Spanish, factors that have made it quite distinct from any other cuisine found in South-east Asia.

The geography of Indonesia

Often described as 'a jewelled necklace' strung between Australia and the mainland of South-east Asia, Indonesia is made up of more than 13,500 islands, only some of which have names, and includes Java, Bali, Sumatra, parts of Borneo and parts of New Guinea.

Home to 245 million people, Indonesia ranks as the sixth largest population in the world. Despite this, less than 1,000 of the islands are populated, as some are too small or too barren to sustain any form of settlement. In fact, the distribution of people is so uneven that the city of Java is inhabited by over 80 million people – one third of the total population of the entire archipelago.

The physical geography and the climate of this island archipelago have an important bearing on the food. Floods and volcanic eruptions frequently tear up the earth, resulting in very fertile soil and a lush green landscape. Apart from the cooler mountain peaks and high volcanic craters that are the backbones of most of the major islands, many of the islands function like greenhouses under the steamy heat.

Rice grows majestically in splendid, architecturally-perfect hillside terraces in Bali and Java; cassava grows wild on the slopes of Java's Mount Merapi; tea plantations adorn the scenery in western Java; papaya trees sprout like weeds on Sumatra; and the tropical fishing in the crystal-clear waters off Lombok is incredible in its diversity and abundance. By contrast, the highlands of West Irian Jaya see small harvests of sweet potato and the craggy hills of Nusa Tengarra are only good for growing corn.

To experience Indonesian food at its best, Java is perhaps the place to be as it is home to a wealth of agricultural produce and many inspired, tasty dishes. A plate of rice is transformed into a feast for all the senses. The pungent spices recall a history of trade and invasion, and the fiery chilli, which appears on every plate, reflects the warm spirit of the people.

Below *The islands of Indonesia spread across the base of South-east Asia.*

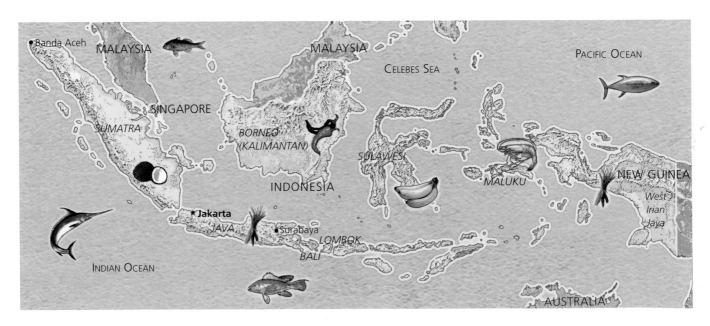

Right *The Philippines – a cluster of islands almost set apart from the rest of South-east Asia.*

The geography of the Philippines

The islands of the Philippines, situated approximately 500 miles south-east of the Asian continent, are more compact than the islands that make up Indonesia. The principal group of islands are called the Visayas and they are situated between Luzon to the north, Palawan to the west, and Mindanao to the south. With their palm-fringed beaches and stunning reefs, the islands of Cebu and Boracay are among the main hotspots of the Visayas.

However, since many of the islands are yet to be discovered by tourists, much of the Philippines remain a traveller's secret paradise. In this diverse ecosystem, there are triumphant rice terraces, dense tropical jungles, cascading waterfalls, deserted pearly beaches and steep mountains with active volcanoes. On the small island of Bohol, you can also discover the delicious-sounding Chocolate Hills –

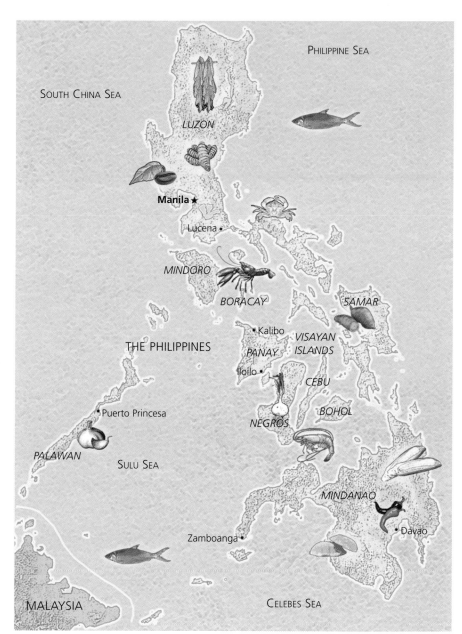

1268 nearly identical hills on which dense vegetation roasts in the dry season to a rich chocolate brown.

In the remote hills, there are still a few indigenous tribes clinging to their ancient customs; a stark contrast to the more fashionable centres, which feature American music, coffee shops and fast food. Inhabiting this blend of East and West are some of the friendliest people on Earth. Their giggly *joie de vivre* is infectious and flows though every vein of the culture. A glorious tradition of feasting accentuates the merriment, and one thing you can say with certainty is that the Filipinos love to eat. In fact they eat so often and with such relish that you could be excused for thinking that's all they do!

Left *According to an old Filipino legend, the Chocolate Hills are the solidified teardrops of a local giant.*

The history and landscape of Indonesia

The lush, green islands that comprise modern Indonesia have a long history of invasion and trade with many nations around the world, including Malaysia, China, India, Persia, Arabia and Spain, as well as various European sea powers during the Spice Wars in the sixteenth and seventeenth centuries. This regular and prolonged contact with foreign countries had a profound impact on all facets of life in Indonesia, from farming techniques and religion to ingredients and cooking techniques, and the legacy is still much in evidence today.

Indonesian ancestry

Early archaeological research records Java man as a hunter-gatherer who lived on a diet of taro, fruit, fish and game. From around 4000BC successive migrations from South-east Asia wiped out Java man, producing a new Indonesian race predominantly made up of Malays and sea-faring Melanesians.

It wasn't until the spread of the Dongson civilization from Vietnam and southern China around 3000 years ago, however, that significant cultural changes occurred. The arrival of the Dongson heralded the spread of rice and irrigation techniques across the islands, and the introduction of the water

Above *The use of a* kuali *(wok) in this bustling street café in Bali reveals the Chinese influence on the cuisine.*

buffalo as a beast of burden as well as a source of food. The ritual custom of sacrificing the buffalo was also adopted and still exists in Sumatra, Sulawesi and Nusa Tenggara.

By the seventh century BC, well-organized societies existed in the Indonesian archipelago, where people farmed irrigated, green rice paddies and domesticated water buffalo, chickens, pigs and dogs, and village kitchens were stocked with the native breadfruit, bananas, yams and coconuts.

Left *A rice paddy in Bali being tilled using the ancient method of man and a pair of water buffalo.*

Early influences

In its early years, the islands that are now collectively known as Indonesia were heavily influenced by the culinary techniques and ingredients of Malaysia, China, India, Persia, Arabia and Spain.

The Chinese traders and immigrants who visited the islands from the seventh century onwards brought rice, noodles and soy sauce, as well as the stir-frying techniques that have become such an integral part of the cuisine throughout the islands.

Indian, Persian and Arab merchants exchanged their goods for Chinese products and island spices, such as cloves and cinnamon bark. The origin of Indonesian curry, *gulai* or *kare*, can be traced back to these traders, since the cardamom, cumin, coriander and garlic in the dish all came from India.

The Spanish explorers of the sixteenth and seventeenth centuries introduced ingredients from the New World. Suddenly, corn, pineapples and tomatoes were readily available, as well as the ubiquitous chilli pepper, which was quickly absorbed into all facets of the cuisine.

Trade with these countries also brought about a fundamental change to the indigenous belief system, as Hinduism and Buddhism were introduced and widely practised. However, the growth of Islam in the thirteenth century, spreading west to east, eventually took hold of most of the islands, and the satellite kingdoms of the Majapahit were declared independent Muslim states.

In spite of the recurrent presence of European sea powers during the Spice Wars in the sixteenth and seventeenth centuries, the dominance of Islam persisted, infiltrating most pockets of the archipelago and resulting in such a big Muslim population that today it claims to be the largest in the world.

The Spice Wars

Prior to the sixteenth century, European merchants travelled to Venice to acquire spices that had been brought in from Constantinople, where they had been bought from Arab sailors who had visited the "spice islands" of the East Indies (now known as Indonesia).

However, with the price of spices rising, these faraway islands became an irresistible target for European traders who wanted to cash in on the profits. The first to reach the islands were the Portuguese in 1511, when they captured the Malay port of Melaka and made a fortune from the trade in cloves and nutmeg out of Maluku.

The Dutch were the next to reach the East Indies in 1596, heralding the start of the Spice Wars. By 1607 they had defeated the Portuguese and gained control of the clove trade from Maluku and had occupied the Banda Islands for the nutmeg. The English also joined the Spice Wars in 1601, setting sail under the auspices of the East India Company.

A diverse cuisine

Apart from introducing tea, the European sea powers involved in the Spice Wars had little influence on the religious or culinary scene of Indonesia. Instead it was Chinese, Indian, Arab and Persian traders and the Spanish explorers who had a lasting impact.

If we examine modern Indonesian cuisine closely, we can find the threads of this diverse history permeating through many of the dishes. For example, in Aceh and north Sumatra, where many spice traders settled, Indian and Arab spices – such as ginger, pepper, coriander seeds, cumin, cloves, cinnamon, cardamom and fennel – dominate the food. Similarly, throughout the islands, the Chinese tradition of stir-frying, noodles and fried rice are part of the everyday street scene.

Interestingly, the egg-topped national fried rice dish, *nasi goreng*, is one of the few dishes to trace its origins to a European power – Holland. Another Dutch influence is the rice table, *rijsttafel*, which was based on the custom of feasting in villages at the end of the harvest, but which has since evolved into a spread of dishes that is erroneously served in restaurants as an example of classic Indonesian cuisine.

Right *Architecturally beautiful, the terraced rice paddies of Indonesia are a distinctive feature of the landscape.*

Indonesian culinary customs

The Indonesian kitchen is extremely functional and the cooking is a relaxed affair, with simplicity at the core of all the dishes. There is an open-minded attitude towards ingredients and preparation – no strict rules, no right or wrong ingredients, just an understanding that most dishes begin with a spice paste, laced with chillies. Street food is popular in the cities, and most Indonesians eat at least one meal away from home each day. This is not surprising, given the dazzling range of tempting snacks on offer at stalls and from roving vendors on every street.

The daily routine

An Indonesian day starts with breakfast at sunrise, while the temperature is still cool. A familiar morning scene is one of chattering women sitting outside their homes over their bowls of rice topped with chillies and fried shallots.

The traditional breakfast varies from region to region. In Java it might consist of a bowl of rice left over from the day before. In Maluku, breakfast could be a sago cake and a cup of tea, whereas in Surabaya it might be rice porridge with chicken. In one of the large cities, on the other hand, a wealthy person might indulge in a Western-style breakfast with a bowl of cereal and a cup of coffee.

In many households, a large pot of rice is cooked every morning, along with three to four dishes to accompany it. The rice is often par-boiled and drained, then left to steam in the pot until it is light and fluffy. This enables the cook to keep the rice warm for long periods of time while the other dishes, which often include fish or meat, vegetables and a sambal, are laid out on the table and left there all day for people to help themselves to for lunch and supper.

There is no order, or variety, to the courses; the meal is simply what is on the table. In this type of everyday meal, the rice (or any other staple) is the main component of the meal and the other dishes are spooned over it in smaller quantities simply to flavour and moisten the grains. Only the wealthier families indulge in thick curries, fried or grilled (broiled) meat and substantial chicken or fish dishes on a regular basis.

Fast food

Eating outside the home is also common practice and it is not unusual for most Indonesians to eat at least one meal of the day from a street stall. In the

Below *Indonesian meals usually include rice and lots of other small dishes.*

Below *A* kaki-lima, *or roving street vendor, is a commonplace sight in Java.*

Above *Cooking in the street – a woman prepares ingredients to be wrapped in palm leaves, Bali.*

Above *It is customary for Indonesians to eat with the right hand rather than with Western-style utensils.*

bustling cities, business people are often simply too busy to cook. Rural folk who have moved to the city, on the other hand, often live in accommodation that is so basic there is no kitchen, so they too turn instead to the wide variety of snacks available all day long from the street-side food stalls or the roving vendor, *kaki-lima*, which literally means "five feet" – three for the cart and two for the vendor.

These roving vendors very often specialize in just one type of snack. Among the favourites are *nasi goreng*, the much-loved national fried rice dish, and *pisang goreng*, which are sweet, sticky deep-fried bananas.

Indonesian etiquette

Guests are treated with great respect in Indonesia, but there are certain patterns of etiquette that may at first seem a little disconcerting to a foreigner. For instance, a guest may eat alone while the hosts sit and watch. This is regarded as a gesture of hospitality, showing that the guest is the priority. It is important that the guest accepts the food and shows gratitude, but it is best not to eat too much as the remainder will be eaten by the family afterwards. On communal occasions, you should wait until the host has indicated that you can start. In a family, the eldest member will serve themselves first, but a guest may be given permission to jump the queue.

Generally, Indonesians prefer to eat with their hands, so the chopping of ingredients into bitesize pieces prior

to cooking is both traditional and extremely practical. Only the right hand is used to scoop up the sticky rice and other ingredients, and the same hand is used for passing things. The left hand is strictly reserved for another bodily function, so any left-handed people visiting Indonesia have to learn pretty quickly to lead with the right hand.

When not using hands, a fork and spoon are provided, which makes eating easier when there is a sauce. At the end of a meal, it is customary to praise the cook and to clean your teeth with a toothpick, although this must be done while covering your mouth with one hand.

The history and landscape of the Philippines

The Philippines have a long and turbulent history of colonization by various nations, including China, Spain, America and Japan. It was the 400-year period of Spanish rule, however, which had the most impact on the cultural and culinary landscape, and which first drew the disparate island communities together under one banner. Today, this profound influence is much in evidence in the food and religious beliefs of this predominantly Catholic island archipelago, although some traces of the legacy left by other nations can also be felt.

Filipino ancestry

Prior to the *conquista* by the Spanish in the late 1500s, the native people of the Philippines had existed as a series of tribes based on a subsistence economy and animistic beliefs. This pagan world of the South Seas was akin to their sea-faring cousins, the Polynesians, and was completely distinct from the Hindu, Buddhist, Sinified or Islamized world of Asia, which included the islands of neighbouring Indonesia.

The islands were colonized by the Chinese for a brief period in the eleventh century, and were visited throughout history by Chinese, Indian, Malay and other traders. These traders settled on some of the islands and married local girls, adding to the developing culinary pool. The Malay influence is still evident among the Moros of the Luzon and the Bicolanos, both of whom enjoy hot, spicy food in rich coconut milk sauces.

By 1565, the era of the Hispanic-speaking Filipinos had begun. During this period, after a history of being by-passed by its neighbouring cultures, it suddenly became a worthy destination for leisure and trade. With all the food and jewels arriving from places like India, Cambodia and Japan, Manila emerged as the Port of Asia and was finally regarded as Asian.

Spanish influences

During the 400 years of Spanish rule, the Philippines were used as a production base for sugar and other agricultural crops, as well as as a significant trading port within the Spanish empire.

The cultural and physical landscape of the Philippines was transformed by the Spanish, who brought with them not only the Catholic religion, but also corn, sweet potatoes, tomatoes, chillies, cacao, tobacco, papaya, pineapples, guava and avocados from the New World, and cheeses, sausages, hams and olives from Spain.

Left *Piles of corn on the cob are sold at a market in Manila, revealing the strong Spanish influence on Filipino ingredients.*

Above *A typical vegetable stall displaying the season's produce, including pumpkin, aubergine (eggplant) and beansprouts.*

As well as food the Spanish brought art, architecture and engineering and, most important of all, they introduced water buffalo and the plough. Where there had once been recurrent famine on some islands, such as the Visayas, corn and sweet potatoes soon became staples, and the region was able to export rice, sugar, tobacco, coffee, hemp, jute, indigo, pearls, cotton, tortoiseshell, betel nut and spices.

The character of *la cocina Filipina* was cast during the Spanish colonial period, resulting in an interesting blend of Spanish, Malay and Chinese traditions. The strongest of these was the Spanish

Right *Children and young men harvest coconuts, which grow in abundance in the Philippines.*

influence, which is clearly evident in both the ingredients and the names of many dishes, including *arroz caldo* (colonial rice soup), *pochero* (beef and chorizo stew with plantain and chickpeas), *leche flan* (Filipino crème caramel) and the popular *tortilla* made with potatoes or bitter melon.

In fact, the Spanish had such a strong culinary influence that when Chinese cooking methods were widely adopted their provenance was disguised by Creole names, such as *pancit guisado* (stir-fried noodles) and *lumpiang frito* (fried spring rolls).

The irreversible strength of the Spanish culinary influence was due to the *guisado*, a simple process of sautéing ingredients to garnish the food that every proud Filipino cook swears by. This practice has resulted in the creation of many of the classic dishes including *adobo* (chicken and pork cooked with vinegar and chickpeas), *guisadong*

Right *Children and young men harvest coconuts, which grow in abundance in the Philippines.*

ampalya at itlog (Spanish-style omelette with bitter melon) and *tinolang manok* (chicken and ginger broth with papaya).

Armed with these new skills and their own sense of taste, these simple-living people were thrust into a world of haute cuisine under their Spanish rulers, who demanded elaborate menus worthy of visiting royalty and other distinguished guests, and would dine in style with fine wines and sherry.

By the nineteenth century, the Filipinos had become such skilful cooks that entire towns and provinces became renowned for their local culinary art. Some peoples, such as the Pampango and Visayan, were considered gourmets, attracting visitors from far and wide.

Left *Leche flan, one of the most famous Spanish-influenced desserts.*

American influences

In the late nineteenth century, the United States took over the Philippines and granted it independence after the end of World War II. The Americans brought with them the US education system, resulting in a high literacy rate in English, although the native Tagalog and Colonial Spanish are spoken in schools too.

Despite this, the American influence on the culinary scene was minimal and the distinct Hispanic influence is still very much in evidence in *la cocina Filipina* and the town *fiestas*. The American legacy is only really recognizable in the national use of spoken English; the street food, where well-known global fast food outlets selling fried chicken and burgers are commonplace; and in the Westernized youth cultures of music and fashion.

Filipino culinary customs

The food culture of the Philippines is generally a healthy one that is based on a lot of rice, fresh fish and a wide range of seasonal vegetables, which include both indigenous ingredients and those that were brought over by settlers. A typical Filipino day will include an average of five meals – breakfast; morning *merienda* (snack); lunch; afternoon *merienda* and dinner. There are numerous feasts throughout the year, all of which give the Filipinos every excuse to indulge their passion for making and consuming large amounts of delicious food.

The daily routine

As in the rest of South-east Asia, rice is the staple food of the Philippines and is served with almost every dish. Fried rice is popular for breakfast, served with dried fish or *longaniza*, the local spicy pork sausages, spiked with black pepper and garlic. Fried eggs are popular for breakfast too, as are continental-style breads, coffee and hot chocolate.

Although the morning *merienda* is referred to as a snack, it can range from something as simple as a few slices of refreshing watermelon to a substantial bowl of stir-fried noodles, spring rolls or even an assortment of savoury sandwiches and sweet, sticky rice cakes.

Lunch and supper tend to be big meals in the Philippines. Among the wealthy, these meals may include four or five courses, comprising a soup, followed by fresh fish and then a meat dish, fresh fruit and finally, if dining Spanish-style, a rich, sweet dessert.

Between lunch and supper there is yet another *merienda*, which consists of sandwiches, cakes and tea, but also spring rolls (*lumpia*), noodles (*pancit*) and a few local sweet dishes made from coconut milk, glutinous rice, pineapple or other tropical fruits.

Typical foods and techniques

Traditionally, roasting, steaming and sautéing are the main methods used for cooking fish and meat. Fish is also marinated in sour flavours which are sourced naturally from fruits such as tamarind, guava and kalamansi limes.

Salty flavours are derived from the national fermented fish sauces, *patis* and *bagoong*, and from Chinese soy sauce, whereas the sweet notes come from blocks of natural palm sugar. Meat, though much sought after, is eaten less frequently because of the cost. However, when it comes to fiestas and family celebrations, no expense is spared and every imaginable meat dish is cooked.

At a meal, food is often laid out buffet-style in a colourful display. The indigenous Spanish-influenced dishes are often quite heavy on the stomach, but interspersed among them are lighter dishes, such as prawns (shrimp) and vegetables in a tamarind-flavoured broth, and tangy seaweed and papaya salads.

Thanks to the Spanish, bread plays an important role in Filipino meals, where it is called *pain de sal* and is made with

Left *A stall selling sacks of rice, potatoes, pineapples, citrus fruit and bananas.*

salt, sugar and wheat flour to produce a spongy baked bun that is dipped in hot coffee or tea.

Apart from the baguettes of Vietnam and the Western loaves of Hong Kong and Singapore, the daily appearance of bread in the Philippines is quite unusual in South-east Asia, where rice tends to be the staple that is served with every meal.

Water is usually served with a meal, although wine goes well with Filipino dishes that are not too spicy.

Traditional dishes

The names of many Filipino dishes denote the cooking style or the ingredients used in the dish. For example, *adobo*, a dish originating from Mexico and now, arguably, the national dish of the Philippines, always refers to pork or chicken, or a combination of the two, cooked gently in vinegar, ginger, garlic and black pepper.

Sinigang, adapted from delicate Japanese soups, refers to meat or fish simmered in a sour-flavoured broth, which is often garnished with the flowers of the tamarind tree. *Kinilaw* is a dish of fresh fish or shellfish marinated in vinegar or kalamansi lime juice and spices, and *inihaw* refers to a dish of grilled (broiled) meat or fish.

Other traditional Filipino dishes include *guinataan* in which meat, fish or vegetables are cooked in coconut milk; *pesa*, which consists of plain boiled fish seasoned with plenty of fresh root ginger and black pepper; *diniguan*, which combines the internal organs of a pig or chicken with the blood; *pipian*, a chicken or pork dish that is brightly coloured by fried annatto seeds and thickened with ground peanuts; and *kari-kari*, a beef stew that can be made with the shin (shank) or the tail.

Above *Women preparing Filipino classics at a festival stall. Dishes are called by their English names, revealing the extent to which it has become the main language.*

Etiquette and hospitality

In some of the outlying islands and rural areas of the Philippines the traditional custom of eating with the fingers still persists but, in the cities, the Filipinos usually eat Western-style with plates and cutlery.

Filipinos are particularly hospitable people, and visitors to the islands are often treated to a fabulous range of cooked dishes and fresh fruit, often served on simple bamboo tables in the shade of rooves made from woven banana leaves.

Cities like Manila and Cebu are particularly renowned for both the variety and excellence of their dishes and restaurants, where almost every regional cuisine is available. In Pampanga, the specialities are *tocino* (honey-cured pork) and *longaniza* (sausages), and the cuisine of the Bicol region, based on chillies and coconut milk, is famous for its spicy flavour and rich, creamy sauces, exemplified by dishes such as *laing* (taro leaves simmered in spiced coconut milk) and *bicol express* (a fiery pork dish).

Religious and festival food

Both Indonesians and Filipinos celebrate domestic and religious events with food. In Indonesia, Muslims mark holy events, such as *Ramadan* or *Idul Adha,* with fasting or the consumption of traditional foods, such as goat. Hindu communities prepare lavish feasts for family events, such as births, marriages, and deaths, as well as routinely creating elaborate edible offerings for their gods. Similarly, in the Philippines, Catholics have fiestas in every town in honour of their patron saints, as well celebrating traditional Catholic dates such as Easter and Christmas.

Indonesian celebrations

Throughout its history, Indonesia has been heavily influenced by religions such as Animism (the belief that everything has a soul), Buddhism, Hinduism and Islam, and ritual celebrations are common affairs.

Food is such an essential part of these festivities that there is a special name for a meal prepared for a lot of people, *selamatan.* This is usually a domestic event to mark a family occasion, such as the birth of a child, a birthday, moving house, harvesting, circumcisions and funerals. This type of meal will include a variety of meat, chicken and egg dishes positioned around the *tumpeng*, a pyramid of yellow rice, the tip of which is offered to the eldest guest.

Meat, especially traditional dishes such as *rendang* (slow-cooked buffalo or beef in coconut milk), is always served at celebratory feasts. In Bali, a feast may revolve around a spit-roast pig, although this Hindu island is an exception as 90 per cent of the population of Indonesia is Muslim and does not eat pork.

Depending on the wealth of a family, a wedding can range from a small affair to a communal feast. This lasts for several days and consists of a large buffet-style spread, which usually includes a spit-roast pig or goat. At a Javanese wedding, the bride feeds the groom by hand to symbolize her new role.

In Java, there is also a feast for the seventh month of pregnancy, which involves seven dishes and seven hard-boiled eggs, one of which is skewered and placed in the central rice dish. It is believed that if the feast is elaborate and beautifully presented, the birth of a girl will be predicted, whereas an unremarkable presentation of dishes will signify a boy.

Muslim festivals

For the majority of Indonesians, the principal celebrations are *Ramadan*, the Muslim month of fasting, and *Idul Adha*. During the month of *Ramadan*, which falls on the ninth month of the Muslim calendar, the devout are forbidden to let anything pass through

Above *A festive meal in Indonesia, consisting of small dishes arranged around the* tumpeng, *or rice pyramid.*

their lips between sunrise and sunset. Many street stalls and eateries are shut for this period as a mark of respect. However, once the sun has set there is the sound of drums beating and the faithful being called to prayer, and meat and vegetable dishes and mounds of rice are brought out and eaten communally.

The end of the month of fasting is called *Lebaran* or *Idul Fitri* and is a time when many Indonesians visit their families to ask forgiveness for any wrongdoings, and to drink sweetened black tea and sticky rice cakes. Little

Above *It is quite common in Indonesia to stumble across small offerings of food and flowers left out for the gods.*

coconut-leaf packets of steamed rice, *ketupat*, are hung up as decoration and symbols of goodwill.

The other important date on the Muslim calendar is *Idul Adha*, which commemorates the near-sacrifice of Isaac. As is traditional in Muslim cultures all over the world, a sheep or goat is sacrificed to mark the event and the meat is shared among the family or community to be cooked in various ways.

Idul Adha takes place 70 days after *Idul Fitri* and is easily recognizable, since the hapless sacrificial beasts are much in evidence as they are transported live to the market in the family car, in the backs of pick-up trucks or strapped onto the backs of bikes.

Hindu festivals

On the island of Bali, the lively and colourful Hindu calendar is celebrated with spicy regional dishes. These celebrations include *Kedaso*, the

festival of the tenth full-moon, and *Penampahan*, a festival of purification, when pigs are sacrificed to the gods.

However, every day can seem like a festival in Bali where the culinary life flows freely in markets brimming with delectable produce, and in the streets, which are peppered with busy food stalls. Wherever a god or spirit may reside, there are offerings of fresh fruit and specially cooked food.

Often these offerings are beautifully presented and can include carefully designed towers of fruit, spoonfuls of rice artistically displayed in banana-leaf pouches, and fancy shaped rice cakes. Whether these offerings are in a rice paddy, a bus station or in a doorway, it is essential that you carefully step around them and leave them untouched.

Sacrificial offerings are also scattered along the edges of rice paddies to keep the demons away, and there is often a

shrine to the Hindu goddess of rice and harvest, *Dewi Sri*, who is presented with fresh fruit and flowers.

Other elaborate food offerings, which may include home-grown vegetables and whole chickens, are made for the anniversary of the founding of a local Hindu temple, when processions of immaculately dressed women make their way to the temple with the beautiful foods carefully balanced on their heads. Once the gods have devoured what they need, the leftovers are shared amongst the community. Generally, at such temple celebrations, the gender roles are quite clearly defined, as the men do all the cooking and the women prepare the spices.

Below *A procession of Hindu women carry carefully stacked and very elaborate offerings for the gods in Bali.*

Filipino religious beliefs

Although Hinduism reached the distant outpost of Bali, it never spread as far as the Philippines. Similarly, Buddhism was carried across much of South-east Asia but managed to miss the Philippines.

In fact, the Philippines managed to escape most of the spreading religions, including the cults and philosophies of China and the Shinto and Zen beliefs of Japan. The only religion that did arrive in the Philippines was Islam in 1475, but it only really managed to get as far as Mindanao, a lush volcanic island in the south of the Philippines, which is now quite dangerous to visit as it has become a stronghold for Islamic terrorists. The Muslim minority of the Philippines celebrate Ramadan and *Idul Adha* with fasting and feasting in the same way as other Muslims in Asia.

The Spanish conquerors, on the other hand, stayed in the Philippines for 400 years, an occupation that inevitably had a lasting impact on cultural life. As a result, Filipinos embraced the Catholic faith, making the Philippines the only Christian country in Asia. With the faith came religious festivals and festive dishes, which are mainly of Spanish origin but with a native twist.

Filipino fiestas and feast days

There are plenty of occasions to celebrate in the Philippines, as the festivals range from religious and communal get-togethers to the full-blown, week-long Mardi Gras, *Ati-Atihan*, which rivals the carnival in Rio de Janeiro for vibrancy and takes place in towns such as Kalibo, Badan and Makato, starting on the third Sunday of January.

Another Mardi Gras-style festival takes place in Iloilo City and celebrates the patron saint, Santo Nino, with a procession of outrageous costumes, dancing and plenty of food. In October, there is a wonderful food festival in Zamboanga city. With street parties, food fairs, open markets, dancing and a regatta with traditional sailboats, this is a colourful extravaganza.

Every town in the Philippines has a patron saint, and each town has a feast day to celebrate its founding anniversary. This means that there is always a fiesta somewhere in the Philippines. Floats are decorated with flowers and images of the village royalty, and people dress in historical costume and hold dancing competitions. Special dishes, such as *adobo* (chicken and pork cooked with vinegar and ginger), are prepared and shared among neighbours to signify the gathering together of a community.

Left *A colourful and vibrant street procession at the* Ati-Atihan *carnival in Kalibo, the Philippines.*

Left *Edible decorations made from rice and food colouring are exhibited during the annual harvest feast in the Philippines.*

Left *Edible decorations made from rice and food colouring are exhibited during the annual harvest feast in the Philippines.*

status symbol. New Year welcomes the abundance of produce in the coming year. To mark the occasion, Filipinos prepare satay and fruit salads, which include more expensive fruits, such as grapes and apples, and there are lantern processions and fireworks in every village.

Easter is the main Christian festival in the Philippines, and it is the one that Filipinos look forward to the most since everyone goes to the beach with lots of food to share. During the Holy Week, when the Filipinos fast for five days, they are only allowed to eat fish and vegetables in the morning and evening. Between 12 noon and 5pm, they must fast, and at no time during the five days can they eat meat. With such dietary restrictions on a nation that constantly thinks about food, the feasting on the Sunday, the Day of the Resurrection, is inevitably spectacular. There is always a suckling pig roasting on a spit, as well as other many other pork dishes.

Christian festivals and holy days, such as Christmas, the Lunar New Year, Lent and Easter, are also flamboyant occasions, and are celebrated with a great deal of feasting.

Many of the festive foods on these occasions are Spanish in origin, and include savoury favourites, such as *pochero* (beef and chorizo stew with plantain and chickpeas), and sweet dishes, such as *leche flan* (Filipino crème caramel). Chinese-inspired noodle dishes, such as *pancit guisado* (stir-fried noodles), *pancit luglog* (noodle soup) and *pancit molo* (a Filipino version of wonton soup), are also popular festive dishes.

For All Saints Day on 1 November families gather at the local cemetery to give the crypts a fresh coat of paint and to feast on the favourite dishes of the deceased, snacking and celebrating long into the night by the gravesides, to the sound of guitars.

Christmas and New Year are great occasions for celebrating with food. Generally, if a Filipino lives near a beach, the fiesta will take place there. Lots of pork and chicken dishes, such as *aroz valenciana* (Filipino risotto with stir-fried liver), *paella* and *adobo* are prepared, as well as a spit-roast suckling pig and vast quantities of rice cakes.

Wealthy Filipinos sometimes choose to have spaghetti as a special meal for Christmas, as pasta is regarded as a

Right *The Filipinos are a pork-loving nation. Here, rows of plum pigs are displayed at a market.*

The kitchen and essential flavours

Most South-east Asian culinary cultures, including Indonesia, are based on ancient Chinese philosophy. This includes the balance of opposites (*yin* and *yang*), which means that all ingredients must blend harmoniously on the plate, yet retain their distinct flavours. The presence of five principal flavour notes – salty, bitter, sour, spicy and sweet – also plays an important role in every meal. Interestingly, while the the flavour notes are important in Filipino cuisine cooking, the *yin yang* philosophy is not.

A taste of Indonesia

A melting pot of diverse cultures and traditions, Indonesia has experienced a rich and varied history, which is epitomized in its stunning cuisine.

Receptive and adaptable, the Indonesians have consistently absorbed the new, such as pineapple and chillies, and blended it with the old, creating a wide selection of exotic dishes to suit every taste.

Classic Indonesian dishes are often of peasant origin and use simple ingredients. These include *gado gado*, a dish of raw and cooked vegetables served in a peanut and coconut milk sauce; *tempe*, a fermented tofu cake which is generally cooked in broth or stir-fried; and the ubiquitous, fiery *sambal*, a condiment made with lots of chillies, which tends to be served with everything.

These traditional dishes can vary slightly from region to region according to local preferences and the availability of the key ingredients.

Indonesian implements

Usually very basic, the main kitchen utensils include cleavers, chopping boards, wire ladles and a grinding stone made from volcanic rock, which leaves the paste that is made in it with a slightly coarse texture.

Many of the utensils are handmade and practical, such as the ladles made from halved coconut shells. A wok (*kuali* or *wajan*) is the main cooking pot for all types of cooking. Terracotta fireplaces are traditional and often fuelled by coconut husks. Every Indonesian kitchen possesses a coconut scraper. Chopsticks are used in Chinese communities, but generally forks or spoons are used for soupy rice and noodle dishes and fingers are used for everything else. Believed to make the food taste better, only the fingertips of the right hand are used and finger bowls are provided.

Traditional ingredients

A typical Indonesian kitchen will revolve around the *sembako*, the nine essentials: rice, sugar, eggs, meat, flour, corn, cooking oil, salt and gas fuel.

Palm sugar, made by extracting and boiling the sap from palm trees, is the primary sweetener in Indonesian cooking. It is sold in thick blocks, which are piled high in the markets, and amounts are chipped off as and when needed. Sugar extracted from the cane is also used, particularly as an instant sweetener, and is sprinkled over fried bananas or stirred into tea.

Left *Traditionally, Indonesian women cook over a wood fire in their relatively basic kitchens.*

The sour notes in Indonesian food tend to emanate from tamarind, which is sold in dried or paste form in the markets, and is used liberally to cut the oiliness of a dish.

Frequent features in the basic Indonesian kitchen are banana leaves and fresh coconuts. The multi-purpose banana leaves are used for wrapping food that is going to be steamed or roasted, for wrapping soya beans and yeast together to make tempeh, or as a serving vessel or plate. Although coconut milk and other coconut products are available, the fresh coconut is preferred.

The most popular cooking fuel is coconut oil, which is used for all types of cooking and is often preferred for deep-frying because of its lingering taste. Other types of oil commonly used include peanut oil and corn oils.

Pastes and sambals

No Indonesian dish is complete without its pungent pastes and fiery *sambals*. Foremost among these is the ubiquitous national shrimp paste, *terasi belacan*. It is made from small shrimp that are rinsed in sea water and then dried, salted and dried again before being pummelled into a paste. This is then left for two weeks to dry out before it is shaped into blocks and

Coconut Oil

A feature of South east Asian dishes, coconut oil is much richer than peanut oil and lends its coconut flavour to the food. To make coconut oil, gently boil coconut cream in a pan until the milk evaporates and all that is left is rich, clear oil. 225g/8oz/ 1 cup coconut cream makes about 50ml/2fl oz/¼ cup oil.

wrapped in paper to encase the smell. As with many South-east Asian cultures, this paste adds an essential salty and fishy taste to almost every dish.

At the start of many dishes there is the *bumbu*, which is a base paste made up of crushed spices such as cumin, coriander seeds, cardamom, turmeric, shallots, garlic, ginger, lemon grass, cinnamon and chillies, which is moistened by coconut milk or stock to make a paste.

One of the popular spice pastes in Bali and Java is the elaborate *base gede*, which is made by pounding garlic, shallots, galangal, chillies, lemon grass and turmeric along with candlenuts and shrimp paste, which is then used as the principal flavouring in a number of seafood, poultry and meat dishes.

The Indonesian *sambal* is an invaluable condiment that is essential to the enjoyment of an Indonesian meal. It is designed to go with almost anything, but is particularly good at

Above *Indonesian shrimp paste is fermented in the sun for two weeks.*

livening-up grilled (broiled) or deep-fried fish and for lifting the gamey taste of roasted goat.

Bottles of *sambal* can be bought at South-east Asian stores but freshly made versions are far more interesting as they can contain a variety of ingredients. The base ingredients are always chillies, garlic, shallots and salt, but other variations, such as *sambal badjak*, can include shallots, sugar, tamarind, galangal and shrimp paste, or *sambal jeruk*, which contains lime juice, lime rind, chillies, salt and vinegar.

The most ubiquitous sambal of all is *sambal terasi*, made with chillies, lime and shrimp paste. The word *sambal* also refers to something fried with lots of chillies, such as *sambal cumi-cumi*, (squid cooked in a hot chilli sauce), which is then served with yet more *sambal*.

Herbs and spices

With such an abundance of indigenous barks, leaves and roots, the Indonesian kitchen is rich in spices, such as galangal, turmeric, kaffir lime leaves, the twisted pandanus (screwpine), cinnamon bark, cumin and coriander seeds, lemon grass and cloves. The cloves are spread out at the side of roads and left to dry, and are more often destined for the clove-flavoured cigarettes than for any particular dish.

In parts of Indonesia, such as Sumatra, where there is a history of Arab and Indian traders, there is a complex use of local spices but, throughout the region, it is the chilli that rules the roost. An Indonesian dish without chillies in it, or accompanying it, is almost unthinkable!

The Indonesians are so addicted to chillies that they appear in the *bumbu* at the beginning of a meal, in a *sambal* at the end, or simply in their raw, fresh form to chew on between mouthfuls during the meal. In fact, chillies are so entrenched in the culinary psyche that it is easy to forget that chillies are one of the New World ingredients that only arrived in the region in the sixteenth century.

Tamarind Water

The tamarind fruit is brown and shaped like a broad (fava) bean pod. The sticky pulp is contained within the pod and easily extracted with a spoon. To make tamarind water, soak the fresh or dried tamarind pulp in 60ml/4 tbsp boiling water for 5 minutes. Break it up with a fork and press it through a sieve (strainer) to extract the flavoured water.

Above *Everyday spices in Indonesian cooking include cardamom, star anise, cinnamon bark and cloves.*

Above *The ubiquitous hot, fresh, red chillies are piled high at a local vegetable market in Surabaya, Java.*

A taste of the Philippines

Due to the long period of Spanish rule, the food of the Philippines differs from that of the rest of South-east Asia primarily in that it does not rely heavily on herbs and spices. The exception to this is Bicolano food, which is based on coconuts and finger chillies.

Filipino food is founded instead on ginger, onion, and garlic, combining the cooking methods of the colonial Spaniards with the traditional dishes of the indigenous island people and their local ingredients. The result is a hearty and simple cuisine that makes good use of innards and oxtail, as well as insects and crickets from the rice paddies.

The Spanish style of *la cocina Filipina* makes the most of an interesting mix of local ingredients, which are often sautéed and casseroled, and it is customary to use Western utensils. A rounded pan, the *carajay*, which is shaped like a wok, is used for stir-frying ingredients, such as vegetables and noodles, but the majority of the cooking is done in frying pans and casseroles.

The Filipinos also enjoy a fiery burst of chillies but they are not always included in the dish. Instead hot Thai chillies, or finger chillies as they known in the Philippines, will be offered in their natural form to chew on, or they will be chopped finely and used to spike the beloved coconut vinegar that is splashed on to everything and offered as a dip.

The Bicolano people of the Luzon are the most similar to the Indonesians in their use of chillies and coconut milk. Regarded by other Filipinos as chilli-mad, they apparently love them so much that they tolerate the persistent typhoons that tear up their houses as long as the chilli plants remain standing in the ground!

Sauces and marinades

The Filipinos have their own version of shrimp paste, which is called *bagoong*. More of a sauce than a paste, the fermented *bagoong* is sold in bottles in which you can actually see the tiny shrimp or anchovies floating. The sauce is a greyish, opaque colour with a very strong smell and is an acquired taste.

Dearly treasured by Filipinos, *bagoong* is more often reserved for particular dishes, such as *pinakbet* (aubergine, bitter melon and okra stew), whereas the pungent, national fish sauce, *patis*, is splashed in to almost everything. Both are available in Southeast Asian and Chinese markets but, as an alternative, you can substitute *bagoong* with Chinese anchovy sauce.

Filipinos frequently draw on the Spanish legacy of marinades. Ingredients are often marinated in coconut vinegar, ginger and garlic before cooking, and raw ingredients such as oily fish and shrimp are cured in lime juice and coconut vinegar, as is exemplified in the national favourite *kinilaw* (Filipino cured herring).

Sweet and sour

Herbs and strong spices are used sparingly in Filipino cooking, which relies mainly on garlic, ginger and bay leaves for flavouring. The Filipino penchant for sweet and sour notes is achieved by combining coconut vinegar or kalamansi lime juice with palm or cane sugar, as in *adobo* (chicken and pork cooked with vinegar and ginger), the national dish, which originally hailed from Mexico.

When Filipinos talk about their beloved vinegar they mean coconut vinegar, which is cloudy white and made from coconut palm sap. Generally, they prefer to cook with coconut oil for its flavour, or with groundnut or corn oils for frying.

Garnishes

Both the Indonesian and Filipino cultures strive for balance in their meals and regard the finishing touches as extremely important. Garnishes, such as fried shallots, spring onions (scallions) and sprigs of coriander (cilantro) are not just for decorative purposes, they are very much part of the dish as a whole and should not be omitted.

Dips, sauces and *sambals* are equally important, and are considered crucial to the whole enjoyment of a particular dish. For example, the Filipino spring rolls, *lumpia*, would be regarded as naked and dull without coconut vinegar dipping sauce, just as the popular *bakmie goreng* (Indonesian stir-fried noodles) and *nasi goreng* (Indonesian stir-fried rice) would lack their desired Indonesian touch if the ever-popular *kecap manis*, the thick, sweet soy sauce, was omitted.

Above *Cloudy coconut vinegar and salty, tangy* patis *are used during cooking and are splashed on to almost everything.*

When it comes to street food, however, traditions can go haywire in some areas, as tomato ketchup appears with increasing frequency in the more Americanized bars and stalls.

Right *Satay stalls are very popular at open-air markets all over the Philippines.*

Basic recipes

Makes enough to flavour 1–2 dishes

2 shallots, finely chopped

2 garlic cloves, finely chopped

25g/1oz fresh galangal,
finely chopped

25g/1oz fresh turmeric, chopped

4 red chillies, seeded and chopped

1 lemon grass stalk, chopped

5ml/1 tsp ground coriander

2.5ml/½ tsp ground black pepper

30–45ml/2–3 tbsp palm or
vegetable oil

10ml/2 tsp *terasi* (Indonesian
shrimp paste)

10ml/2 tsp palm sugar

Balinese spice paste
Base gede

The founding spirit of Balinese cooking, *base gede* appears in its various
guises throughout Indonesia. It forms the basis of many meat, poultry and
fish dishes and can be used as a marinade to rub all over meat that is to be
grilled. Variations include candlenuts, tamarind and extra chillies. Deliciously
pungent, it is a very handy spice paste to have ready in the refrigerator.

1 Using a mortar and pestle, grind the shallots, garlic, galangal, turmeric, chillies and
lemon grass to a coarse paste. Beat in the coriander and black pepper.

2 Heat the oil in a small heavy-based pan, stir in the paste and fry until fragrant and
beginning to colour. Stir in the *terasi* and sugar and continue to fry for 2–3 minutes,
until darker in colour. Remove from the heat and leave to cool.

3 Spoon the spice paste into a jar, cover and store in the refrigerator for up to 1 week.

Per Portion Energy 158kcal/654kJ; Protein 6.6g; Carbohydrate 8.9g, of which sugars 7.5g; Fat 13.6g, of which saturates 1.3g; Cholesterol 25mg; Calcium 126mg; Fibre 0.8g; Sodium 355mg.

Chilli and shrimp paste
Sambal terasi

There is a saying in Indonesia: "If your eyes do not water, the food is not good", which gives you some idea of the fieriness of this paste, which is served with everything.

Serves 4

15–30ml/1–2 tbsp palm, groundnut (peanut) or vegetable oil

2 shallots, finely chopped

3 garlic cloves, finely chopped

4 spring onions (scallions), finely chopped

8 red Thai chillies, seeded and finely chopped

10–15ml/2–3 tsp *terasi* (Indonesian shrimp paste)

1 Heat the oil in a small wok or heavy-based pan. Stir in the shallots, garlic, spring onions and chillies and fry until fragrant and beginning to colour.

2 Add the *terasi* and continue to fry for about 5 minutes, until dark and blended. Remove from the heat and leave to cool.

3 Spoon the spice paste into a jar, cover and store in the refrigerator for up to 1 week.

Per Portion Energy 46kcal/191kJ; Protein 2.6g; Carbohydrate 2.2g, of which sugars 1.3g; Fat 3g, of which saturates 0.4g; Cholesterol 13mg; Calcium 44mg; Fibre 0.5g; Sodium 111mg.

Kalamansi sauce
Sawsawan kalamansi

This popular Filipino dipping sauce can be served with anything but is particularly good with fish and rice dishes.

Serves 4

2 kalamansi limes

60ml/4 tbsp *patis* (fish sauce)

1 Squeeze the juice from the limes and put in a small bowl. Add the *patis* and beat together until thoroughly blended.

2 Spoon the sauce into a jar, cover and store in the refrigerator for up to 1–2 days.

Per Portion Energy 8kcal/33kJ; Protein 0.5g; Carbohydrate 1.5g, of which sugars 1.4g; Fat 0g, of which saturates 0g; Cholesterol 0mg; Calcium 4mg; Fibre 0g; Sodium 1068mg.

Tamarind and lime sauce
Sampaloc at kalamansi

This popular hot and sour dipping sauce is usually prepared for freshly grilled fish or steamed shellfish.

Serves 4

2 kalamansi limes

30ml/2 tbsp tamarind paste

2 spring onions (scallions), white parts only, finely chopped

2 red chillies, seeded and finely chopped

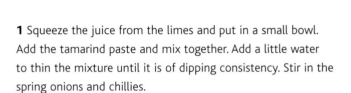

1 Squeeze the juice from the limes and put in a small bowl. Add the tamarind paste and mix together. Add a little water to thin the mixture until it is of dipping consistency. Stir in the spring onions and chillies.

2 Spoon the sauce into a jar, cover and store in the refrigerator for up to 1 week.

Per Portion Energy 6kcal/23kJ; Protein 0.6g; Carbohydrate 0.6g, of which sugars 0.6g; Fat 0.1g, of which saturates 0g; Cholesterol 0mg; Calcium 10mg; Fibre 0.2g; Sodium 6mg.

Coconut vinegar sauce
Sukat bawang sawsawan

This spicy dipping sauce is perfect with certain foods, such as steamed shellfish, spring rolls and fried chicken.

Serves 4

60–75ml/4–5 tbsp coconut vinegar

3 red chillies, seeded and finely chopped

4 spring onions (scallions), white parts only, finely chopped

4 garlic cloves, finely chopped

1 Spoon the vinegar into a small bowl. Add the chillies, spring onions and garlic and mix well together.

2 Spoon the sauce into a jar, cover and store in the refrigerator for up to 1 week.

Per Portion Energy 21kcal/85kJ; Protein 1.8g; Carbohydrate 2.2g, of which sugars 0.7g; Fat 0.3g, of which saturates 0g; Cholesterol 0mg; Calcium 14mg; Fibre 0.6g; Sodium 4mg.

Indonesian peanut sauce
Sambal kacang

Also known as *bumbu sate*, this is a very popular dipping sauce for fried and grilled meats and steamed vegetables. *Sambal kacang* is closely related to the peanut sauces of Malaysia, Vietnam and Thailand, and is always available at street stalls. To make an authentic Indonesian peanut sauce, the peanuts must be very finely ground, which can be done in a blender.

1 Heat the oil in a heavy-based pan, stir in the shallot and garlic and fry until golden brown. Add the ground peanuts, *terasi* and sugar and continue to fry for 3–4 minutes, until the peanuts begin to colour and release some of their oil.

2 Stir in the tamarind paste, *kecap manis* and chilli powder. Add the water, bring it to the boil then simmer for 15–20 minutes, until the sauce has reduced and thickened – small deposits of oil may appear on the surface. Remove the pan from the heat and leave the mixture to cool.

3 Pour the mixture into an electric blender or food processor and blend to form a smooth sauce. Spoon into a jar, cover and store in the refrigerator for up to 1 week.

Serves 4

15–30ml/1–2 tbsp groundnut (peanut) or vegetable oil

1 shallot, finely chopped

2 garlic cloves, finely chopped

150g/5oz/¾ cup plus 30ml/ 2 tbsp unsalted peanuts, finely ground

15ml/1 tbsp *terasi* (Indonesian shrimp paste)

15ml/1 tbsp palm sugar

15ml/1 tbsp tamarind paste

15ml/1 tbsp *kecap manis* (Indonesian sweet soy sauce)

5ml/1 tsp chilli powder

300ml/½ pint/1¼ cups water

Per Portion Energy 309kcal/1284kJ; Protein 14g; Carbohydrate 10.9g, of which sugars 7.5g; Fat 23.6g, of which saturates 4.2g; Cholesterol 19mg; Calcium 77mg; Fibre 3g; Sodium 431mg.

Soups and soupy stews

Soups and soupy stews

The soups of South-east Asia range from thin, clear liquids designed to cleanse the palate to the more meaty dishes that can be served on their own as a snack or light meal. Soups are not always served at the beginning of a meal and they are nearly always served with rice, which is moistened by generous spoonfuls of the hot liquid. Indonesian soups are usually served with a spicy *sambal* on the side, and perhaps some wedges of fresh lime. Filipino soups are often served with a splash of coconut vinegar over the top, garnished with spring onions (scallions) or fresh herbs, such as basil or parsley, and accompanied by fresh chillies to chew on for an added fiery kick.

The key to all the tasty soups of this region is a really good, well-flavoured stock made with pork, chicken and beef bones as well as pungent ingredients such as peppercorns, ginger, lemon grass stalks, fish sauce and soy sauce. Fish stocks will include the fish head, dried fish and shellfish, and the discarded shrimp shells, which are cooked together in a large pot before being strained through a colander. The large ingredients are pressed against the colander when straining the stock in order to obtain maximum flavour.

The quality of the stock is of particular importance when it is used in regional clear soups, which are often served as palate cleansers to cut the grease from oily dishes, or to whet the appetite at the beginning of the meal. It is considered important that these refreshing broths contain the five flavour notes of South-east Asian cooking – salty, sweet, sour, bitter and spicy.

In Indonesia, the soups generally fall into three categories; *sop*, *soto* and *sayur*. The traditional *sop* is a clear, Chinese-inspired broth that is generally served as a palate cleanser or spooned over noodles to both moisten and lightly flavour them. The meaty, substantial *soto*, on the other hand, is often served as a light meal on its own or as a snack between meals at hawker stalls.

The most popular national soup is *soto ayam* (Indonesian chicken broth with fried potatoes), which is readily available at many street stalls all over the country. Regional favourites include *soto bandung*, a beef and vegetable soup from Bandung; *soto macassar*, a spicy soup made with offal; and *soto madura*, a fragrant beef and lime soup flavoured with ginger. All these soups are served with rice and most Indonesians will have a little chilli *sambal* on the side and wedges of lime to refresh the broth.

Above, from left to right *Aubergines (eggplants); chicken and ginger broth with papaya (tinolang manok); fresh papaya.*

Another popular soup that falls into this category is *bakso*, the beloved national meatball dish, which usually contains noodles and beansprouts and, sometimes, chicken feet. Many Indonesians have a favourite *bakso* seller, who they visit regularly to quench their need for this comfort food.

The *sayur* dishes fall somewhere between a soup and a stew. Referred to as "wet" dishes, these thick and sustaining soups form part of the everyday fare both in the home and at hawker stalls. They usually employ a variety of vegetables as well as meat or fish, although some versions are entirely vegetarian. Spooned over rice, these *sayur* dishes are often designed to moisten and flavour the rice rather than form the basis of the meal. This moist rice can then either be served on its own with dried meat or dried fish and a chilli *sambal*, or as an accompaniment to other dishes.

In the Philippines, where the Spanish-style meals often follow a more rigid course structure, a light soup is normally served as an appetizer, or as a first course, whereas the meatier soups are served as meals on their own for the morning or afternoon *merienda*.

As Filipino meals can be quite rich and sweet, sour-flavoured soups are especially popular. The sour notes are generally obtained from tamarind fruit, kalamansi limes or a local fruit called *kamias*, which resembles the Asian starfruit (carambola), but is small and lime green in colour. The collective name for many sour soups is *sinigang*, which comes in many guises, including the infamous Bicolano version, which is laced with chillies and made creamy and rich with the addition of coconut milk. One of the most popular sour soups is *sinigang na baboy* (pork and vegetable soup).

The *tinolo* soups are palate-cleansing clear broths, often Japanese-influenced, with thin slices of green papaya or green mango floating in the steaming liquid, and garnished with papaya flowers. One of the most delightful soups on offer in the Philippines is the delicate *binacol na manok*, traditionally made with chicken and the sweet, jelly-like flesh of a young, green coconut. The local *buko* coconut is particularly sought after for this soup as its soft flesh and internal water are deliciously sweet.

Chinese-influenced soups appear in the Philippines too. Perhaps the best known of these is the noodle dish *pancit palabok* (celebration noodles), which is often prepared for birthdays and family occasions. At street stalls, the dish is always stir-fried, which is why the recipe appears in the rice, noodles and spring rolls section of this book, but in some households it is served as a soupy stew instead.

In general, the soups of Indonesia and the Philippines are rich in variety and are all well worth trying, even if some of the ingredients, such as tripe, initially seem unpleasant or unfamiliar. There are soups for all occasions, ranging from thin, light broths such as *tinalong manok* (chicken and ginger broth with papaya) to thick, hearty soups packed with delicious vegetables and meat, such as *sayur terung* (spicy aubergine (eggplant) soup with beef and lime).

Above, from left to right *Indonesian chicken broth* (soto ayam)*; tamarind pods; spicy aubergine soup with beef and lime* (sayur terung).

Pumpkin, snake bean and bamboo soup with coconut
Sayur lemeng

This tasty soup is from Java, where it is served on its own with rice or as an accompaniment to a poached or grilled fish dish. In some parts of Java, the dish includes small prawns but, if it is packed with vegetables alone, it makes an extremely satisfying vegetarian meal. Generally, *sayur* dishes are accompanied by a chilli *sambal*, which can be made by pounding chillies with shrimp paste and lime juice, or with ginger and garlic.

Serves four

30ml/2 tbsp palm, groundnut (peanut) or corn oil

150g/5oz pumpkin flesh

115g/4oz snake beans (yardlong beans)

220g/7½oz can bamboo shoots, drained and rinsed

900ml/1½ pints coconut milk

10–15ml/2–3 tsp palm sugar

130g/4½oz fresh coconut, shredded

salt

For the spice paste

4 shallots, chopped

25g/1oz fresh root ginger, chopped

4 red chillies, seeded and chopped

2 garlic cloves, chopped

5ml/1 tsp coriander seeds

4 candlenuts, toasted and chopped

To serve

cooked rice

chilli *sambal*

1 To make the spice paste, using a mortar and pestle, grind all the ingredients together to form a smooth paste, or whiz them together in an electric blender or food processor.

2 Heat the oil in a wok or large, heavy pan, stir in the spice paste and fry until fragrant. Toss the pumpkin, snake beans and bamboo shoots in the paste and pour in the coconut milk. Add the sugar and bring to the boil. Reduce the heat and cook gently for 5–10 minutes, until the vegetables are tender.

3 Season the soup with salt to taste and stir in half the fresh coconut. Ladle the soup into individual warmed bowls, sprinkle with the remaining coconut and serve with bowls of cooked rice to spoon the soup over and a chilli *sambal*.

Cook's tip Bamboo shoots are available in cans in most Chinese and South-east Asian markets and stores and large supermarkets.

Variation When pumpkins are not in season, use a different member of the squash family, such as butternut squash or acorn squash.

Per Portion Energy 333kcal/1388kJ; Protein 6g; Carbohydrate 26g, of which sugars 23.8g; Fat 23.6g, of which saturates 11.7g; Cholesterol 0mg; Calcium 115mg; Fibre 4.9g; Sodium 258mg.

Spicy aubergine soup with beef and lime
Sayur terung

A delicious soupy stew from North Sumatra, this soup can be made with aubergines, green jackfruit or any of the squash family. For an authentic meal, serve the soup with a bowl of rice and a chilli *sambal*, bearing in mind that the quantity of rice should be greater than the soupy stew, as the role of the soup is to moisten and flavour the rice.

1 To make the spice paste, using a mortar and pestle, grind all the ingredients together to form a textured paste, or whiz them together in an electric blender or food processor.

2 Heat the oil in a wok or heavy pan, stir in the spice paste and fry until fragrant. Add the beef, stirring to coat it well in the spice paste, then add the coconut milk and sugar. Bring the liquid to the boil, then reduce the heat and simmer gently for 10 minutes.

3 Add the aubergine wedges and kaffir lime leaves to the pan and cook gently for a further 5–10 minutes, until tender but not mushy. Stir in the lime juice and season with salt to taste.

4 Ladle the soup into individual warmed bowls and serve with bowls of cooked rice to spoon the soup over, wedges of lime to squeeze on the top and a chilli *sambal*.

Cook's tip As there are a variety of aubergines (eggplants) available in different parts of the world, which come in many different shapes and sizes, just use your judgement about how much you need and ensure the flesh is cut into bitesize chunks.

Serves four

30ml/2 tbsp palm, groundnut (peanut) or corn oil

150g/5oz lean beef, cut into thin strips

500ml/17fl oz/generous 2 cups coconut milk

10ml/2 tsp sugar

3–4 Thai aubergines (eggplants) or 1 large Mediterranean aubergine, cut into wedges

3–4 kaffir lime leaves

juice of 1 lime

salt

For the spice paste

4 shallots, chopped

4 red Thai chillies, seeded and chopped

25g/1oz fresh root ginger, chopped

15g/½oz fresh turmeric, chopped or 2.5ml/½ tsp ground turmeric

2 garlic cloves, chopped

5ml/1 tsp coriander seeds

2.5ml/½ tsp cumin seeds

2–3 candlenuts

To serve

cooked rice

1 lime, quartered

chilli *sambal*

Per Portion Energy 224kcal/938kJ; Protein 12.1g; Carbohydrate 14.6g, of which sugars 12.6g; Fat 13.6g, of which saturates 3.2g; Cholesterol 22mg; Calcium 79mg; Fibre 3g; Sodium 181mg.

Spicy tripe soup with lemon grass and lime

Soto babat

This popular Indonesian soup is packed with spices and the refreshing flavours of lemon grass and lime. Steaming bowls of *soto babat* are sought after at food stalls as a great pick-me-up. The locals prefer their tripe to be chewy for this spicy soup, which is served with a pungent chilli *sambal*, but if you prefer, you can cook it for longer so that the tripe is tender.

Serves four

250ml/8fl oz/1 cup rice wine vinegar

900g/2lb beef tripe, cleaned

2 litres/3½ pints/8 cups beef stock or water

2–3 garlic cloves, crushed whole

2 lemon grass stalks

25g/1oz fresh root ginger, finely grated

3–4 kaffir lime leaves

225g/8oz mooli (daikon) or turnip, finely sliced

15ml/1 tbsp palm, groundnut (peanut) or vegetable oil

4 shallots, finely sliced

salt and ground black pepper

For the *sambal*

15ml/1 tbsp palm, groundnut (peanut) or vegetable oil

2 garlic cloves, crushed

2–3 hot red chillies, seeded and finely chopped

15ml/1 tbsp chilli and shrimp paste

25ml/1½ tbsp tomato paste

Cook's tip If you prefer your tripe tender, cook it for 4–5 hours and increase the quantity of stock.

1 Fill a large pan with about 2.5 litres/4½ pints/11¼ cups water and bring it to the boil. Reduce the heat and stir in the vinegar. Add the tripe, season with salt and pepper and simmer gently for about 1 hour.

2 Meanwhile, prepare the *sambal*. Heat the oil in a small, heavy pan. Stir in the garlic and chillies and fry until fragrant. Stir in the chilli and shrimp paste then add the tomato paste and mix until thoroughly combined. Tip the paste into a small dish and put aside.

3 When the tripe is cooked, drain and cut into bitesize squares or strips. Pour the stock or water into a large pan and bring it to the boil. Reduce the heat and add the tripe, garlic, lemon grass, ginger, lime leaves and mooli or turnip. Cook gently for 15–20 minutes, until the mooli or turnip is tender. (For tender tripe, omit the mooli or turnip at this stage, simmer the tripe for 4–5 hours and then add the mooli or turnip for the last 15 minutes of cooking).

4 Meanwhile, heat the oil in a small frying pan. Add the shallots and fry for about 5 minutes until golden brown. Drain on kitchen paper.

5 Ladle the soup into individual warmed bowls and sprinkle the shallots over the top. Serve the soup with the spicy *sambal*, which can be added in a dollop and stirred in.

Per Portion Energy 160kcal/668kJ; Protein 19.2g; Carbohydrate 5.5g, of which sugars 4.8g; Fat 7g, of which saturates 1.1g; Cholesterol 163mg; Calcium 198mg; Fibre 1.9g; Sodium 299mg.

Indonesian chicken broth
Soto ayam

This is perhaps the most popular of all Indonesian soups. Throughout South-east Asia you will find variations of this soup; even in Indonesia it varies from region to region, such as the Bali version that includes noodles instead of potatoes. Colourful and crunchy, this classic soup can be served as an appetizer or as a light and refreshing dish on its own.

1 First prepare the ingredients for serving by putting the coriander, spring onions, chillies and lime wedges into a serving bowl.

2 Heat the oil in a heavy pan, stir in the ginger, turmeric, lemon grass, kaffir lime leaves, candlenuts, garlic, coriander seeds and *terasi* and fry until the mixture begins to darken and become fragrant. Pour in the chicken stock, bring to the boil, then reduce the heat and simmer for about 20 minutes.

3 Meanwhile, heat the oil for deep-frying in a wok. Add the potato slices and fry until crisp and golden brown. Remove from the pan with a slotted spoon, drain on kitchen paper and put aside.

4 Strain the flavoured chicken stock and reserve. Pour back into the pan and season with salt and pepper to taste. Return to the boil, then reduce the heat and add the chicken. Simmer for 2–3 minutes until cooked but still tender.

5 Quickly prepare four to six soup bowls by sprinkling some of the cabbage and bean sprouts into the base of each. Ladle the broth over the cabbage and bean sprouts, dividing the chicken equally between the bowls, and arrange the sliced boiled eggs and deep-fried potatoes over the top.

6 Serve the hot broth with the ingredients for serving, so that each diner can add them to their own bowls, and pass around the *kecap manis* to drizzle over the top.

Serves four to six

30ml/2 tbsp palm, groundnut (peanut) or corn oil

25g/1oz fresh root ginger, finely chopped

25g/1oz fresh turmeric, finely chopped, or 5ml/1 tsp ground turmeric

1 lemon grass stalk, finely chopped

4–5 kaffir lime leaves, crushed with fingers

4 candlenuts, coarsely ground

2 garlic cloves, crushed

5ml/1 tsp coriander seeds

5ml/1 tsp *terasi* (Indonesian shrimp paste)

2 litres/3½ pints/8 cups chicken stock

corn or vegetable oil, for deep-frying

2 waxy potatoes, finely sliced

350g/12oz skinless chicken breast fillets, thinly sliced widthways

150g/5oz leafy green cabbage, finely sliced

150g/5oz mung bean sprouts

3 hard-boiled eggs, thinly sliced

salt and ground black pepper

To serve

1 bunch fresh coriander (cilantro) leaves, roughly chopped

2–3 spring onions (scallions), finely sliced

2–3 hot red or green chillies, seeded and finely sliced diagonally

2 limes, cut into wedges

kecap manis (Indonesian sweet soy sauce)

Variation Instead of waxy potatoes, you could try using finely sliced sweet potato, yam or plantain.

Per Portion Energy 296kcal/1238kJ; Protein 21.1g; Carbohydrate 14.8g, of which sugars 3g; Fat 17.5g, of which saturates 2.8g; Cholesterol 136mg; Calcium 63mg; Fibre 2.7g; Sodium 96mg.

Chicken and ginger broth with papaya
Tinolang manok

Serves four to six

15–30ml/1–2 tbsp palm or groundnut (peanut) oil

2 garlic cloves, finely chopped

1 large onion, sliced

40g/1½oz fresh root ginger, finely grated

2 whole dried chillies

1 chicken, left whole or jointed, trimmed of fat

30ml/2 tbsp *patis* (fish sauce)

600ml/1 pint/2½ cups chicken stock

1.2 litres/2 pints/5 cups water

1 small green papaya, cut into fine slices or strips

1 bunch fresh young chilli or basil leaves

salt and ground black pepper

cooked rice, to serve

In the Philippines, this is a traditional peasant dish that is still cooked every day in rural areas. In the province of Iloilo, located in the Western Visayas, green papaya is added to the broth, which could be regarded as a Filipino version of *coq au vin*. Generally the chicken and broth are served with steamed rice, but the broth is also sipped during the meal to cleanse and stimulate the palate.

1 Heat the oil in a wok or a large pan that has a lid. Stir in the garlic, onion and ginger and fry until they begin to colour. Stir in the chillies, add the chicken and fry until the skin is lightly browned all over. Pour in the *patis*, stock and water, adding more water if necessary so that the chicken is completely covered. Bring to the boil, reduce the heat, cover and simmer gently for about 1½ hours, until the chicken is very tender.

2 Season the stock with salt and pepper and add the papaya. Continue to simmer for a further 10–15 minutes, then stir in the chilli or basil leaves. Serve the chicken and broth in warmed bowls, with bowls of steamed rice to ladle the broth over the top.

Variation Young chilli leaves, plucked off the chilli plant, are added at the end to spike the soup with their unique flavour. There is no similar substitute for these leaves, but if you don't have any, you can use fresh basil instead.

Per Portion Energy 290kcal/1219kJ; Protein 46.4g; Carbohydrate 9.8g, of which sugars 8.7g; Fat 7.5g, of which saturates 1.5g; Cholesterol 169mg; Calcium 40mg; Fibre 2.2g; Sodium 150mg.

Serves four to six

2 litres/3½ pints/8 cups pork or chicken stock, or a mixture of stock and water

15–30ml/1–2 tbsp tamarind paste

30ml/2 tbsp *patis* (fish sauce)

25g/1oz fresh root ginger, finely grated

1 medium yam or sweet potato, cut into bitesize chunks

8–10 snake beans (yardlong beans)

225g/8oz kangkong (water spinach) or ordinary spinach, well rinsed

350g/12oz pork tenderloin, sliced widthways

2–3 spring onions (scallions), white parts only, finely sliced

salt and ground black pepper

Cook's tip Fresh tamarind pods, packaged tamarind pulp and pots of tamarind paste are all available in Middle Eastern, Indian, African and South-east Asian food shops.

Tamarind pork and vegetable soup
Sinigang na baboy

Sour soups, usually flavoured with tamarind or lime, are very popular in South-east Asia. In the Philippines, the national sour soup is *sinigang*, which varies from region to region, such as the Bicolano version made with coconut milk and chillies. However, it can be made with any combination of meat or fish and vegetables as long as it is sour. Tamarind pods or *kamias*, a sour fruit similar in shape to star fruit, are the common souring agents as most Filipinos grow them in their gardens.

1 In a wok or deep pan, bring the stock to the boil. Stir in the tamarind paste, *patis* and ginger, reduce the heat and simmer for about 20 minutes. Season the mixture with salt and lots of pepper.

2 Add the yam and snake beans to the pan and cook gently for 3–4 minutes, until the yam is tender. Stir in the spinach and the sliced pork and simmer gently for 2–3 minutes, until the pork is just cooked and turns opaque.

3 Ladle the soup into individual warmed bowls and sprinkle the sliced spring onions over the top.

Per Portion Energy 126kcal/532kJ; Protein 14g; Carbohydrate 12.3g, of which sugars 4.1g; Fat 2.7g, of which saturates 0.9g; Cholesterol 37mg; Calcium 31mg; Fibre 2g; Sodium 417mg.

Colonial rice soup with pork and roasted garlic

Arroz caldo at baboy

Made with pork or chicken, this warming and sustaining rice soup combines the ancient traditions of the Filipino rice culture with the Spanish colonial culinary techniques of browning and sautéing.

1 Heat the oil in a wok or deep, heavy pan that has a lid. Stir in the onion, garlic and ginger and fry until fragrant and beginning to colour. Add the pork and fry, stirring frequently, for 5–6 minutes, until lightly browned. Stir in the peppercorns.

2 Meanwhile, put the rice in a sieve (strainer), rinse under cold running water until the water runs clear, then drain. Toss the rice into the pan, making sure that it is coated in the mixture. Pour in the stock, add the *patis* and bring to the boil. Reduce the heat and partially cover with a lid. Simmer for about 40 minutes, stirring ocassionally to make sure that the rice doesn't stick to the bottom of the pan. Season with salt to taste.

3 Just before serving, dry-fry the garlic in a small, heavy pan, until golden brown then stir it into the soup. Ladle the soup into individual warmed bowls and sprinkle the spring onions over the top. Serve the chillies separately, to chew on.

Serves four to six

15–30ml/1–2 tbsp palm or groundnut (peanut) oil

1 large onion, finely chopped.

2 garlic cloves, finely chopped

25g/1oz fresh root ginger, finely chopped

350g/12oz pork rump or tenderloin, cut widthways into bitesize slices

5–6 black peppercorns

115g/4oz/1 cup plus 15ml/1 tbsp short grain rice

2 litres/3½ pints/8 cups pork or chicken stock

30ml/2 tbsp *patis* (fish sauce)

salt

To serve

2 garlic cloves, finely chopped

2 spring onions (scallions), white parts only, finely sliced

2–3 green or red chillies, seeded and quartered lengthways

Per Portion Energy 195kcal/813kJ; Protein 14.8g; Carbohydrate 19.9g, of which sugars 3.4g; Fat 6.2g, of which saturates 1.3g; Cholesterol 37mg; Calcium 24mg; Fibre 0.8g; Sodium 399mg.

Serves four to six

2 litres/3½ pints/8 cups fish stock

250ml/8fl oz/1 cup white wine

15–30ml/1–2 tbsp tamarind paste

30–45ml/2–3 tbsp *patis* (fish sauce)

30ml/2 tbsp palm sugar

50g/2oz fresh root ginger, grated

2–3 red or green chillies, seeded and finely sliced

2 tomatoes, skinned, seeded and cut into wedges

350g/12oz fresh fish, such as trout, sea bass, swordfish or cod, cut into bitesize chunks

12–16 fresh prawns (shrimp), in their shells

1 bunch fresh basil leaves, roughly chopped

1 bunch flat leaf parsley, roughly chopped

salt and ground black pepper

To serve

60–90ml/4–6 tbsp coconut vinegar

1–2 garlic cloves, finely chopped

1–2 limes, cut into wedges

2 red or green chillies, seeded and quartered lengthways

Cook's tip You can shell the prawns (shrimp) if you would prefer to, but the shells add to the flavour of the soup.

Hot and sour filipino fish soup
Sinigang na isda

Chunky, filling and satisfying, the Filipino fish soups are meals in themselves. There are many variations on the theme, depending on the region and the local fish, but most are packed with shellfish, flavoured with sour tamarind combined with hot chilli, and served with coconut vinegar flavoured with garlic. Served on its own or with rice, this soup certainly awakens the senses!

1 In a wok or large pan, bring the stock and wine to the boil. Stir in the tamarind paste, *patis*, sugar, ginger and chillies. Reduce the heat and simmer for 15–20 minutes.

2 Add the tomatoes to the broth and season with salt and pepper. Add the fish and prawns and simmer for a further 5 minutes, until the fish is cooked.

3 Meanwhile, in a bowl, quickly mix together the coconut vinegar and garlic for serving and put aside.

4 Stir half the basil and half the parsley into the broth and ladle into individual warmed bowls. Garnish with the remaining basil and parsley and serve immediately, with the spiked coconut vinegar to splash on top, the lime wedges to squeeze into the soup, and the chillies to chew on for extra heat.

Per Portion Energy 137kcal/576kJ; Protein 17.7g; Carbohydrate 8.1g, of which sugars 8g; Fat 1g, of which saturates 0.1g; Cholesterol 92mg; Calcium 76mg; Fibre 1.3g; Sodium 644mg.

Street snacks and satay

Street snacks and satay

Snacking is big business in South-east Asia and the Indonesians and Filipinos excel at it. Whether it is at food stalls by the side of the street or in busy shopping malls and food halls, a huge variety of freshly cooked snacks and chargrilled satay is available all day long. Much of the food is deep-fried, cooked on a barbecue or quickly stir-fried, and the assorted aromas that fill the air on a daily basis make the mouth water.

Indonesians are accustomed to eating out. At least one meal of the day is usually consumed at a food stall or eatery of some description. In the cities there are many different ones to choose from, ranging from the *kaki-lima*, the makeshift juice and snack vendor, and the *warung*, the day and night street stalls, to a variety of cafés and restaurants. The crammed, smog-ridden city of Jakarta is known as *Kota Kompor*, the city of stove-burners, as there are so many *kaki-lima* and *warung* to feed the hungry population that you practically trip over burners as you walk through the streets.

As snacking is such big business, there are snacks for every occasion and from every region, including such delicacies as *pisang goreng* (deep-fried bananas sprinkled with sugar), *tahu isi* (fried tofu stuffed with beansprouts and vegetables), and *perkedel jagung* (spicy corn patties), which can be made with corn or potato.

Deep-frying is the usual method of cooking at the Indonesian street stalls, where vast cauldrons of hot oil produce snacks such as *kerupuk* (prawn (shrimp) crackers), *tempe goreng* (crispy fried tempeh) and the all-time favourite, *ayam goreng* (Indonesian street chicken), the unbeatable fried chicken.

Deep-fried *emping* is an Indonesian speciality, made from the red seeds of the fruit from the *Melinjo* tree. First, the seeds are roasted to release the kernels, which are then flattened, dried and fried in oil. Served hot, straight from the pan, and coated in a chilli sauce, *emping* are sought after at the night stalls. Deep-fried chips, made from purple yams and cassava, bananas or fish skin, are also popular with hungry passers-by.

Perhaps the most traditional of all cooking methods – roasting skewered meat over charcoal – satay is one of the most readily available street dishes in both Indonesia and the Philippines. However, in Indonesia, where there are more

Above, from left to right *Peanut crackers* (rempeyak kacang)*; tempeh; meatballs with roasted coconut* (rempah).

satay stalls than any other type of eatery, it could be regarded as an institution. The pungent smoke from the hot grills (broilers) wafts around the streets, particularly in the evening. Business is brisk and the meat is often served in the form of a takeaway meal. Cars and bicycles will stop briefly beside a satay stall, wait until the meat is cooked, then drive away with a collection of sticks and rice wrapped in paper.

Any meat or shellfish can be used for satay, ranging from the commonplace lamb, chicken and pork satay to rabbit, horse, prawns (shrimp), innards, snake and lizard, as well as the Filipino speciality *toyong pusit satay*, which is made with dried squid.

Generally, Indonesian satay is served with the tangy *sambal kecang* (chilli and shrimp paste) and rice, or *longtong* (rice steamed in banana leaves). In both Indonesia and the Philippines, coconut husks are often used as the cooking fuel on the barbecue, adding their own aroma to the flavour of the cooked meat.

It's not surprising that the Filipinos have such a friendly disposition, since they have the institution of the *merienda*, with designated snacking and resting times. First there is the mid-morning *merienda*, to satisfy that pang of hunger between breakfast and lunch, followed by the mid-afternoon *merienda*, which keeps the body functioning until dinner in the evening.

Although merienda means 'snack', do not be fooled into thinking this will simply be a biscuit (cookie) and a cup of tea, as a Filipino 'snack' can consist of a bowl of *bihon*, stir-fried

rice noodles, or a chunky fish stew and, when the weather is stiflingly hot, juicy watermelon and pineapple may be added to the list. Of course, this amount of food requires a little time to be digested, so the average Filipino and Filipina emerges from the *merienda* both satisfied and well rested.

In the Philippines, the most basic eating place is called a *turo turo*, literally meaning "point point", which is exactly what you do when you spot the dishes you would like to eat. To suit the appetites of this carnivorous nation, the assortment of dishes on display will usually be meat-based, such as crispy *pata* (crackling pork knuckles) and *kaldereta* (Spanish-style lamb stew with green olives). This popular dish can also be made with beef, and you will find the recipe for this version in the meat and poultry section of this book.

Another popular street eatery is the *ihaw ihaw* stall, which offers Filipino versions of grilled (broiled) meat and seafood satay. One of the few vegetable dishes to appear in the street stalls is *pinakbet* (aubergine (eggplant), bitter melon and okra stew), which is flavoured with *bagnet* (crispy fried pork belly), which can be found in this chapter, along with *bagoong*, a fermented anchovy sauce. The recipe for *pinakbet* can be found in the vegetable dishes and salads chapter.

In the big cities, such as Manila, the street food also includes Spanish-style omelettes and paella, as well as many Chinese, Korean and Malay specialities. There is also an increasing demand for a number of Western snacks, such as slices of pizza and burgers with ketchup.

Above, from left to right *Shrimp and scallop satay* (sate lilit)*; peanuts; spicy corn patties* (perkedel jagung).

Peanut crackers
Rempeyek kacang

Deep-fried in vast cauldrons, baskets of *rempeyek* are always on the go as a quick snack in the streets or to nibble with a drink at the beach. Along with prawn crackers, *rempeyek* could be considered Indonesia's answer to fried potato crisps, although they are infinitely more tasty. At many restaurants and formal dinner parties, *rempeyek* are often offered as a welcoming appetizer to take the edge off your hunger while you wait for your meal.

1 Put the rice flour, baking powder, ground turmeric and ground coriander into a bowl. Make a well in the centre, pour in the coconut milk and stir to mix together, drawing in the flour from the sides. Beat well to make a smooth batter.

2 Add the peanuts, candlenuts and garlic and mix well together. Season with salt and pepper then put aside for 30 minutes.

3 Meanwhile, in a small bowl, prepare the seasoning by mixing the paprika or fine chilli flakes with a little salt.

4 Heat a thin layer of oil in a wok or large frying pan and drop in a spoonful of batter for each cracker – the size of spoon doesn't matter as *rempeyak* vary in size. Work in batches, flipping them over when the lacy edges become crispy and golden brown. Drain on kitchen paper and toss them into a basket.

5 Sprinkle the paprika mixture over the crackers and toss them lightly. Serve immediately while still warm and crisp with some chilli *sambal*, if you like.

Variation If you are allergic to peanuts or simply do not like their flavour, you can adapt the recipe and use other nuts, such as almonds and walnuts, or roast some soaked, drained chickpeas and use them instead.

Serves four to five

225g/8oz/2 cups plus 30ml/2 tbsp rice flour

5ml/1 tsp baking powder

5ml/1 tsp ground turmeric

5ml/1 tsp ground coriander

300ml/½ pint/1¼ cups coconut milk

115g/4oz/¾ cup unsalted peanuts, coarsely chopped or crushed

2–3 candlenuts, ground

2–3 garlic cloves, crushed

corn or groundnut (peanut) oil, for shallow frying

salt and ground black pepper

chilli *sambal*, for dipping

To season

5ml/1 tsp paprika or fine chilli flakes

salt

Per Portion Energy 403kcal/1679kJ; Protein 9.7g; Carbohydrate 42.2g, of which sugars 4.6g; Fat 21.3g, of which saturates 3.4g; Cholesterol 0mg; Calcium 44mg; Fibre 2.5g; Sodium 69mg.

Spicy corn patties
Perkedel jagung

When it comes to snack food, fried patties and fritters are as popular as grilled fish and satay at the street stalls in Indonesia. Easy to eat with fingers, the corn patties are often served on a square of banana leaf with fresh lime wedges and a small dollop of chilli *sambal* on the side to give that extra fiery kick to these already quite spicy patties.

Serves four

2 fresh corn on the cob

3 shallots, chopped

2 garlic cloves, chopped

25g/1oz galangal or fresh root ginger, chopped

1–2 chillies, seeded and chopped

2–3 candlenuts or macadamia nuts, ground

5ml/1 tsp ground coriander

5ml/1 tsp ground cumin

15ml/1 tbsp coconut oil

3 eggs

45–60ml/3–4 tbsp grated fresh coconut or desiccated (dry unsweetened shredded) coconut

2–3 spring onions (scallions), white parts only, finely sliced

corn or groundnut (peanut) oil, for shallow frying

1 small bunch fresh coriander (cilantro) leaves, roughly chopped

salt and ground black pepper

1 lime, quartered, for serving

chilli *sambal*, for dipping

1 Put the corn on the cob into a large pan of water, bring to the boil and boil for about 8 minutes, until cooked but still firm. Drain the cobs and refresh under running cold water. Using a sharp knife, scrape all the corn off the cob and put aside.

2 Using a mortar and pestle, grind the shallots, garlic, galangal and chillies to a paste. Add the candlenuts, ground coriander and cumin and beat well together.

3 Heat the coconut oil in a small wok or heavy pan, stir in the spice paste and stir-fry until the paste becomes fragrant and begins to colour. Tip the paste on to a plate and leave to cool.

4 Beat the eggs in a large bowl. Add the coconut and spring onions and beat in the corn and the cooled spice paste until all the ingredients are thoroughly combined. Season the mixture with salt and pepper.

5 Heat a thin layer of corn oil in a heavy frying pan. Working in batches, drop spoonfuls of the corn mixture into the oil and fry the patties for 2–3 minutes, until golden brown on both sides.

6 Drain the patties on kitchen paper and arrange them on a serving dish on top of the coriander leaves. Serve hot or at room temperature with wedges of lime to squeeze over them and a chilli *sambal* for dipping.

Per Portion Energy 368kcal/1531kJ; Protein 10.8g; Carbohydrate 18.1g, of which sugars 8.2g; Fat 28.7g, of which saturates 9.7g; Cholesterol 143mg; Calcium 68mg; Fibre 4.1g; Sodium 196mg.

Crispy fried tempeh
Tempe Goreng

Often cooked at street stalls, this crispy fried tempeh can be served as a snack or as part of a selection of Indonesian dishes. As a snack, tempeh or tofu, which can be cooked the same way, is often served with stir–fried noodles or plain rice and pickled vegetables.

1 Heat 30–45ml/2–3 tbsp of the oil in a wok or large, heavy frying pan. Add the tempeh and stir-fry until golden brown. Using a slotted spoon, transfer the tempeh to kitchen paper to drain.

2 Wipe the wok or frying pan clean with kitchen paper. Heat the remaining 15ml/1 tbsp oil in the wok or pan, stir in the shallots, garlic, galangal and chillies and fry until fragrant and beginning to colour. Stir in the *kecap manis* and toss in the fried tempeh. Stir-fry until the sauce has reduced and clings to the tempeh.

3 Tip the tempeh on to a serving dish and sprinkle with the peanuts and coriander leaves. Serve hot with stir-fried noodles or cooked rice.

Variation Tempeh, which is fermented tofu, can be bought from Chinese and South-east Asian supermarkets. If you are unable to purchase it, then tofu can be used as an alternative.

Serves three to four

45–60ml/3–4 tbsp coconut or groundnut (peanut) oil

500g/1¼lb tempeh, cut into bitesize strips

4 shallots, finely chopped

4 garlic cloves, finely chopped

25g/1oz fresh galangal or fresh root ginger, finely chopped

3–4 red chillies, seeded and finely chopped

150ml/¼ pint/⅔ cup *kecap manis* (Indonesian sweet soy sauce)

30–45ml/2–3 tbsp unsalted peanuts, crushed

1 small bunch fresh coriander (cilantro) leaves, roughly chopped

stir-fried noodles or cooked rice, to serve

Per Portion Energy 258kcal/1071kJ; Protein 14.8g; Carbohydrate 7.7g, of which sugars 5.5g; Fat 18.9g, of which saturates 2.6g; Cholesterol 0mg; Calcium 682mg; Fibre 1.7g; Sodium 2680mg.

Serves four

3 garlic cloves, chopped

40g/1½oz fresh root ginger, chopped

500g/1¼lb pork belly with the rind, cut into thick slabs

3–4 bay leaves

corn, groundnut (peanut) or vegetable oil, for deep-frying

salt and ground black pepper

Crispy fried pork belly
Bagnet

This is a great Filipino treat. Delicious and moreish, the crispy pork can be sliced and eaten as a snack with salad and pickles, or it can be added to salads, soups and vegetable dishes.

1 Using a mortar and pestle, grind the garlic and ginger with a little salt and pepper, until the mixture forms a fairly smooth paste. Rub the paste all over the pork slabs and put them on a plate. Cover with clear film and put in the refrigerator to marinate for at least 1 hour or overnight.

2 Fill a large pan with water and bring to the boil. Add the bay leaves, reduce the heat and slip in the marinated pork slabs. Cook gently for about 1 hour, until the meat is tender but still firm. Using a colander, drain the slabs and leave them in the colander for 30–40 minutes to dry out.

3 Heat enough oil in a wok or pan for deep-frying. Fry the pork for 5 minutes, until they are golden brown. Using a slotted spoon, lift them out and drain on kitchen paper. If eating immediately, slice thinly and serve with rice and pickled vegetables. Alternatively, store in the refrigerator for up to 5 days to use in soups and stews.

Per Portion Energy 576kcal/2377kJ; Protein 19.2g, Carbohydrate 0.1g, of which sugars 0.1g; Fat 55.4g, of which saturates 17.7g; Cholesterol 90mg; Calcium 14mg; Fibre 0.1g; Sodium 97mg.

30ml/2 tbsp groundnut (peanut) or vegetable oil

1 onion, finely chopped

2 garlic cloves, finely chopped

25g/1oz fresh root ginger, finely chopped or grated

50g/2oz pig's fat, finely chopped

225g/8oz pig's liver, chopped

115g/4oz pig's kidney, finely chopped

115g/4oz pig's heart, chopped

15–30ml/1–2 tbsp *patis* (fish sauce)

a handful of fresh chilli leaves or flat leaf parsley, finely chopped, plus extra to garnish

about 8 slices French bread or any crusty rustic loaf

salt and ground black pepper

2 red or green chillies, seeded and quartered lengthways, to serve

Filipino black pudding
Batchoy

Prepared entirely with pig offal, *batchoy* is similar to black pudding, although it is traditionally cooked to a smooth mixture in a pan rather than rolled into a neat sausage. Flavoured with garlic and ginger, *batchoy* is served hot with noodles or rice as a popular street snack at any time of day. In this recipe though, rather than boiling the offal until it becomes soft, the meat is sautéed Spanish-style and served straight from the pan with toasted bread.

1 Heat the oil in a wok or large, heavy frying pan, stir in the onion, garlic and ginger and fry until fragrant and lightly browned. Add the chopped fat and offal and sauté until lightly browned. Stir in the *patis* and chopped chilli leaves or parsley and season with salt and lots of black pepper.

2 Lightly toast the slices of bread. Spoon the sautéed offal on top and garnish with chilli leaves or parsley. Serve as a snack or a light lunch, with the chillies to chew on.

Per Portion Energy 518kcal/2175kJ; Protein 26g; Carbohydrate 56.7g, of which sugars 7g; Fat 22.6g, of which saturates 6.9g; Cholesterol 181mg; Calcium 133mg; Fibre 3.2g; Sodium 893mg.

Filipino street chicken
Peneritong manok

Long before Kentucky-style fried chicken, there was Filipino fried chicken. One of the most popular snacks at the street stalls and a great favourite in the home kitchen, Filipino fried chicken is beautifully brown and crispy with a unique flavour of beer and garlic. The aroma of fried chicken in the streets of Manila and Cebu City is as predominant and enticing as the delectable smells emanating from the satay stalls.

1 Put the chicken pieces in a shallow dish or wide bowl. In a small bowl, add the grated shallots and garlic, season with salt and pepper and mix together. Rub the mixture all over the chicken pieces.

2 In another bowl or jug (pitcher), combine the beer, soy sauce and lime juice and pour the marinade over the chicken. Cover the dish with clear film (plastic wrap) and put in the refrigerator to marinate for at least 6 hours or overnight.

3 In a wok or deep pan, heat enough oil for deep-frying. Fry the chicken in batches until it is rich brown in colour and crispy on the outside. Drain on kitchen paper and serve with cooked rice and salad.

Serves three to four

6–8 chicken pieces, such as breast, thighs or wings

3–4 shallots, grated

3–4 garlic cloves, crushed

450ml/¾ pint/scant 2 cups beer, such as San Miguel, Tiger or Anchor

30ml/2 tbsp light or dark soy sauce

juice of 2–3 kalamansi or ordinary limes

corn or vegetable oil, for deep-frying

salt and ground black pepper

cooked rice and salad, to serve

Per Portion Energy 274kcal/1147kJ; Protein 36.5g; Carbohydrate 1.8g, of which sugars 1.4g; Fat 12.7g, of which saturates 1.7g; Cholesterol 105mg; Calcium 14mg; Fibre 0.2g; Sodium 626mg.

Meatballs with roasted coconut
Rempah

A great favourite at Indonesian buffet spreads and street stalls, these meatballs are versatile and tasty. Moulded into small balls, they can be served as an appetizer with a drink; as a snack dipped in *kecap manis*; or as a main dish with rice and a tangy salad.

1 In a small, heavy pan, dry-fry the coriander and cumin seeds until they give off a nutty aroma. Using a mortar and pestle or electric spice grinder, grind the roasted seeds to a powder.

2 In the same pan, dry-fry the coconut until it begins to colour and give off a nutty aroma. Tip the coconut on to a plate and leave to cool.

3 Heat the coconut oil in the same small, heavy pan, stir in the shallots, garlic and chillies and fry until fragrant and beginning to colour. Tip them on to a plate and leave to cool.

Serves four

5ml/1 tsp coriander seeds

5ml/1 tsp cumin seeds

175g/6oz freshly grated coconut or desiccated (dry unsweetened shredded) coconut

15ml/1 tbsp coconut oil

4 shallots, finely chopped

2 garlic cloves, finely chopped

1–2 red chillies, seeded and finely chopped

350g/12oz lean minced (ground) beef

beaten egg (if necessary)

rice flour, to coat

corn oil, for shallow frying

salt and ground black pepper

To serve

30–45ml/2–3 tbsp freshly grated coconut or desiccated (dry unsweetened shredded) coconut, dry-fried

1 lime, quartered

kecap manis (Indonesian sweet soy sauce)

4 Put the minced beef into a bowl and add the ground spices, dry-fried coconut and shallot mixture. Season the beef mixture with salt and pepper. Using a fork, mix all the ingredients together, adding a little beaten egg, only if necessary, to bind the mixture together.

5 Knead the mixture with your hands and mould it into little balls, not bigger than a fresh apricot. Roll the balls in rice flour to coat them.

6 Heat a thin layer of corn oil in a large frying pan and fry the meatballs for about 5 minutes until they are golden brown all over. Drain on kitchen paper and arrange on a serving dish. Sprinkle the dry-fried coconut over them and serve with the lime wedges for squeezing and *kecap manis* for drizzling over them.

Per Portion Energy 559kcal/2312kJ; Protein 20.2g; Carbohydrate 8g, of which sugars 3.7g; Fat 49.6g, of which saturates 30.4g; Cholesterol 53mg; Calcium 23mg; Fibre 6.3g; Sodium 83mg.

Filipino pork satay
Baboy satay

This is the most popular of all the satay dishes in the Philippines. Pork is the favoured meat and satay is a beautifully simple way of cooking it, so this recipe makes great street, party and picnic food.

1 In a large bowl, mix the oil, soy sauce, *patis*, lime juice, garlic and sugar together to form a marinade. Stir well to ensure the sugar dissolves and season with black pepper.

2 Toss the meat in the marinade, making sure that it is well coated. Cover the bowl with clear film (plastic wrap) and put in the refrigerator for at least 2 hours or overnight. (The longer the pork is marinated the better the flavour).

3 Prepare the barbecue, or, if you are using a grill (broiler), preheat 5 minutes before you start cooking. If using wooden skewers, soak them in water for about 30 minutes. Thread the meat, chorizo and onions on to the skewers and place them on the barbecue or under the hot grill.

4 Cook the satay for 4–5 minutes each side, basting the meat with the marinade occasionally. Serve immediately with rice and a salad or pickled vegetables, and a bowl of coconut vinegar dipping sauce.

Serves 4

30ml/2 tbsp groundnut (peanut) or palm oil

60–75ml/4–5 tbsp soy sauce

15ml/1 tbsp *patis* (fish sauce)

juice of 2–3 kalamansi or ordinary limes

2 garlic cloves, crushed

15ml/1 tbsp palm, granulated or muscavado sugar

500g/1¼lb pork loin, cut into thin bitesize squares

175g/6oz slim chorizo sausage, sliced diagonally

12 baby onions, peeled and left whole

ground black pepper

wooden or metal skewers

To serve

cooked rice

salad or pickled vegetables

coconut vinegar sauce

Per Portion Energy 360kcal/1503kJ; Protein 31.5g; Carbohydrate 11.7g, of which sugars 6.7g; Fat 21.1g, of which saturates 6.8g; Cholesterol 96mg; Calcium 40mg; Fibre 0.6g; Sodium 1048mg.

Dried squid satay

Toyong pusit satay

Dried fish and shellfish are a feature of both South-east Asian cooking and the local markets, where dried squid hangs from poles. In the Philippines, dried fish is usually deep-fried and served with garlic rice, and the dried squid is grilled in the street, luring passers-by with its sweet aroma. Simple and tasty, this dish is often made at the beach and served with iced fruit drinks or chilled *serbesa* (San Miguel beer). It also good served with chunks of bread.

1 Cut each squid into four or five pieces. In a bowl, put the soy sauce, hoisin sauce, peanut butter and lime juice and mix together to form a thick marinade. Toss in the squid pieces, making sure they are well coated and leave to marinate at room temperature for 30 minutes.

2 Meanwhile, prepare the barbecue or, if you are using the grill (broiler), preheat 5 minutes before you start cooking. If using wooden skewers, soak them in water for about 30 minutes. Thread the squid on to skewers.

3 Place the satay on the barbecue or under the grill and cook for 2 minutes on each side, brushing occasionally with any remaining marinade. Serve as an accompaniment to a drink or with chunks of bread and a green mango or papaya salad.

Serves three to four

4–5 whole dried baby squid

30ml/2 tbsp light soy sauce

30ml/2 tbsp hoisin sauce

30ml/2 tbsp smooth peanut butter

juice of 1 kalamansi or ordinary lime

wooden or metal skewers

To serve

green mango or papaya salad

Per Portion Energy 89kcal/374kJ; Protein 9.6g; Carbohydrate 2.2g, of which sugars 1.1g; Fat 4.7g, of which saturates 1.2g; Cholesterol 113mg; Calcium 11mg; Fibre 0.4g; Sodium 615mg.

Spicy shrimp and scallop satay
Sate lilit

One of the tastiest satay dishes, this is succulent, spicy and extremely moreish. Serve with rice and a fruity salad or pickled vegetables and lime.

1 First make the spice paste. Using a mortar and pestle, pound the shallots, garlic, chillies, galangal, turmeric and lemon grass together to form a coarse paste.

2 Heat the oil in a wok or large, heavy frying pan, stir in the paste and fry until it becomes fragrant and begins to colour. Add the *terasi*, tamarind and sugar and continue to cook, stirring, until the mixture darkens. Put aside and leave to cool.

3 In a bowl, pound the shrimps and scallops together to form a paste, or whiz them together in an electric blender or food processor. Beat in the spice paste, followed by the flour and baking powder, and beat until blended. Put the mixture in the refrigerator for about 1 hour. If using wooden skewers, soak them in water for about 30 minutes.

4 Meanwhile, prepare the barbecue, or, if you are using the grill (broiler), preheat 5 minutes before you start cooking. Using your fingers, scoop up lumps of the shellfish paste and wrap it around the skewers.

5 Place each skewer on the barbecue or under the grill and cook for 3 minutes on each side, until golden brown. Serve with the lime wedges to squeeze over them.

Serves four

250g/9oz shelled shrimp or prawns (shrimp), deveined and chopped

250g/9oz shelled scallops, chopped

30ml/2 tbsp potato, tapioca or rice flour

5ml/1 tsp baking powder

12–16 wooden, metal, lemon grass or sugar cane skewers

1 lime, quartered, to serve

For the spice paste

2 shallots, chopped

2 garlic cloves, chopped

2–3 red chillies, seeded and chopped

25g/1oz galangal or fresh root ginger, chopped

15g/½oz fresh turmeric, chopped or 2.5ml/½tsp ground turmeric

2–3 lemon grass stalks, chopped

15–30ml/1–2 tbsp palm or groundnut (peanut) oil

5ml/1 tsp *terasi* (Indonesian shrimp paste)

15ml/1 tbsp tamarind paste

5ml/1 tsp palm sugar

Cook's tip You can use wooden or metal skewers but, if you can find sugar cane or lemon grass stalks, trim them into skewers so that they enhance the dish with their own flavours.

Per Portion Energy 220kcal/922kJ; Protein 27.1g; Carbohydrate 11.5g, of which sugars 1g; Fat 7.3g, of which saturates 1g; Cholesterol 151mg; Calcium 99mg; Fibre 1.5g; Sodium 249mg.

Serves two to four

500g/1¼lb fresh baby squid

30ml/2 tbsp tamarind paste

30ml/2 tbsp chilli sauce

45ml/3 tbsp *kecap manis*
(Indonesian sweet soy sauce)

juice of 1 kalamansi or ordinary lime

25g/1oz fresh root ginger, grated

1 small bunch fresh coriander
(cilantro) leaves

2–4 green chillies, seeded and
quartered lengthways

ground black pepper

To serve

fresh coriander (cilantro) leaves

Variation To make hot, sweet and sour
prawns (shrimp), devein the prawns and
remove the feelers and legs, then rinse,
pat dry, and make an incision along the
tail. Marinate and cook in the same way
as the squid.

Hot, sweet and sour squid
Bakar cumi-cumi asam

The Indonesians and Malays love cooking prawns and squid in this way,
expertly crunching shells and sucking tentacles to savour all the juicy chilli
and tamarind flavouring. Sweetened with the ubiquitous *kecap manis*, the
cooking aroma emanating from these scrumptious squid will make you drool.

1 Clean the squid and remove the head and ink sac. Pull out the backbone and rinse
the body sac inside and out. Trim the head above the eyes, keeping the tentacle
intact. Pat dry the body sac and tentacles and discard the rest.

2 In a small bowl, mix together the tamarind paste, chilli sauce, *kecap manis* and the
lime juice. Beat in the ginger and a little black pepper.

3 Spoon the mixture over the squid and, using your fingers, rub it all over the body
sacs and tentacles. Cover and leave to marinate in the refrigerator for 1 hour.

4 Meanwhile, prepare the barbecue or heat a ridged griddle. Place the squid on the
rack or griddle and cook for 3 minutes on each side, brushing them with the marinade
as they cook. Serve immediately, with fresh coriander leaves.

Per Portion Energy 110kcal/468kJ; Protein 20g; Carbohydrate 2.8g, of which sugars 1.1g; Fat 2.3g, of which saturates 0.5g; Cholesterol 281mg; Calcium 43mg; Fibre 0.6g; Sodium 943mg.

Spanish-style omelette with bitter melon

Guisadong ampalya at itlog

Bitter melon, which is also known as bitter gourd or bitter cucumber, is best when it is young and not too bitter. Believed to aid digestion and strengthen the immune system, bitter melon is often cooked simply in a broth or vegetable stew and is frequently combined with pork and shrimps throughout South-east Asia. Made in the style of a Spanish omelette, this Filipino dish is often enjoyed as a snack, served on a banana leaf with rice or bread.

Serves three to four

450g/1lb bitter melon

30–45ml/2–3 tbsp palm or groundnut (peanut) oil

1 onion, sliced

2–3 garlic cloves, chopped

25g/1oz fresh root ginger, chopped

115g/4oz pork loin, cut into thin bitesize strips

225g/8oz fresh shrimp or small prawns (shrimp), shelled

2–3 tomatoes, skinned, seeded and chopped

1 small bunch chilli leaves or flat leaf parsley, roughly chopped

3–4 eggs, beaten

salt and ground black pepper

1 Fill a bowl with cold water and stir in 10ml/2 tsp salt. Cut the bitter melon in half, remove the spongy core and seeds then cut the flesh into bitesize chunks. Put the melon into the salted water and leave to soak for 30 minutes. Drain, rinse well under cold water then pat dry with kitchen paper before frying.

2 Heat the oil in a large frying pan, stir in the onion, garlic and ginger and fry until fragrant and beginning to colour. Add the pork and fry for 2 minutes.

3 Add the shrimp and fry until they turn opaque, then add the tomatoes and chilli leaves or parsley. Toss in the bitter melon and fry for 3–4 minutes, until tender. Season the mixture with salt and pepper.

4 Pour the eggs over the mixture in the pan, drawing in the sides to let the egg spread evenly. Cover the pan and leave to cook gently until the eggs have set.

5 Serve the omelette hot, straight from the pan, or leave it to cool and serve it at room temperature.

Variation Bitter melon is available in Chinese and South-east Asian markets but if you have trouble finding one, you could use courgette (zucchini) as a substitute.

Per Portion Energy 255kcal/1064kJ; Protein 24.3g; Carbohydrate 10.5g, of which sugars 10.1g; Fat 13.2g, of which saturates 2.7g; Cholesterol 318mg; Calcium 149mg; Fibre 2.7g; Sodium 247mg.

Rice, noodles and
spring rolls

Rice, noodles and spring rolls

The huge influence that the Chinese have had on the culinary culture of South-east Asia is nowhere more apparent than in the tradition of rice, noodles and spring rolls that pervades there. The legacy of early Chinese immigrants is much in evidence in both countries, where rice is the foundation of most meals, and where the name for the rice vermicelli is practically the same: *bihoon* in Indonesia and *bihon* in the Philippines.

Wherever you go in Indonesia, rice shapes the landscape. Stepped, lush green rice paddies drop picturesquely down the hillsides of Sumatra, Java and Bali and sacks of polished rice grains are stacked in the markets. Piled on plates or hidden in sticky savoury and sweet snacks, rice is the foundation of the majority of meals. There is no particular rice season in Indonesia for, as long as there is sufficient rainfall, the paddies flourish continuously with scarecrows positioned at regular intervals to keep birds at bay. The flooded fields of Bali also provide waterways for children to fish for tiny eels, catfish are reared in the paddies until they are big enough for the wok, and domesticated ducks are led out each morning for a swim.

Indonesia has many words for this important commodity. The Indonesian name for a dry rice paddy is *lawang* and, when it is flooded, it is called *sawah*. When the rice is still in its natural state in the paddy, it is called *padi* (the word from which the English "paddy" is derived). Once the rice has been harvested it is called *gabah* and after it has been milled it is referred to as *beras*. The cooked grain is called *nasi*, which is how it appears in all the well-known dishes.

The town of Cianjur in West Java is said to produce the finest long grain rice. Glutinous varieties, such as *ketan* or *pulut*, are destined for savoury and sweet snacks, such as the popular *lemper*, sticky rice cakes filled with a spicy meat mixture. An Indonesian speciality is *ketan hitam*, a black variety, which turns dark purple when cooked, and is also known as 'forbidden rice' because of its colour.

Incredibly versatile, rice is steamed in packages made from woven coconut fronds or banana leaves. It is used to make rice crackers, wrappers, noodles and rice wine, and is the principal ingredient in the national dish, *nasi goreng* (Indonesian fried rice). Plain rice is consumed as a daily filler and rice porridge,

Above, from left to right *Filipino paella* (paella)*; ground turmeric; festive yellow rice* (nasi kuning).

which can be sweet or savoury, is enjoyed for breakfast or as a snack during the day. However, in spite of its versatility and abundance, rice is not the most-favoured staple in all of the islands as taro, cassava and sago are popular in the remoter regions of eastern Indonesia.

The rice terraces of the northern Luzon region of the Philippines are a historical wonder. Built thousands of years ago, they are supported by rock-retaining walls, which also act as an irrigation system, carrying water down from the mountain tops, serving each paddy on the way. For centuries, these terraces have been maintained by the Ifugaos, a northern tribe that has lived in this mountainous region as far back as records go.

There are a number of varieties of rice in the Philippines, but the most valued are the fragrant and aged ones, such as *wag-wag*, as they fluff up easily when cooked. Traditionally, the young, green rice is pounded and roasted to form the powder called *pinipig*, which is used in cakes or sprinkled on to drinks or hot chocolate, whereas the mature grains are soaked overnight and ground into a wet paste, called *galapong*, which is used to give a springy texture to rice cakes and snacks, such as *bilo-bilo*.

For everyday rice, the preference is for the grain to come halfway between the sticky rice of Vietnam and the hard rice of India. Generally, it is washed in several changes of water and simmered in just enough water – up to a finger knuckle depth – until cooked. Once the rice is tender, the pot is often left over the heat to form a crust (*tutong*) on the bottom. This crust is

then lovingly removed from the pot and kept moist overnight, so that it can be fried for breakfast the next day. If a Filipino cook does not want the *tutong*, clay pots are usually lined with banana or pandanus (screwpine) leaves, which also lend their flavour and aroma to the rice. In the Visayas and in Mindanao, rice is cooked and served in little hand-woven baskets made from coconut fronds that hang in bunches in the market.

Rice noodles, wheat noodles, bean thread and egg noodles are all available and used interchangeably in the stir-fried dishes of both countries. If the Indonesians have a preference, it is probably for the sturdier, versatile egg noodles, known as *bakmie*, which form the basis of many popular dishes, such as *bakmie goring* (Indonesian stir-fried noodles). The Indonesians also love to spike their noodles with copious amounts of fresh chilli or chilli oil and sweeten them with a generous splash of *kecap manis* (sweet soy sauce).

The best known Filipino noodle dish is *pancit* (celebration noodles) that is cooked for family celebrations and festive occasions. The word *pancit* is derived from *pansit*, which means something that is easily cooked, and this is true. Usually, egg noodles or the dried wheat noodles are used for this noodle dish, whereas the more delicate rice noodles appear in soups.

The spring rolls found in Indonesia and the Philippines are quite distinct, although both use a crêpe batter for the wrappers, which are filled with interesting ingredients, such as coconut palm heart. Indonesian spring rolls tend to be deep-fried, whereas Filipino ones can be fresh. Both are easy to make.

Above, from left to right *Celebration noodles* (bakmie goreng)*; stir-fried shrimp; Indonesian deep-fried spring rolls* (lumpia goreng).

Festive yellow rice
Nasi kuning

Vibrant yellow and rich in taste, this Indonesian rice dish is only cooked on festive occasions, when it is often heaped up high on a platter to create an impression. Usually made with medium grain rice and coloured yellow with turmeric, this is a stunning rice dish for any occasion.

1 Put the rice in a sieve (strainer), rinse under cold running water until the water runs clear, then drain. Heat the oil in a heavy pan, stir in the shallots and garlic and fry until just beginning to colour. Stir in the rice until coated in the oil.

2 Add the coconut milk, water, turmeric, curry leaves, 2.5ml/ ½ tsp salt and pepper to the pan. Bring to the boil, then lower the heat, cover and simmer gently for 15–20 minutes, until all the liquid has been absorbed.

3 Turn off the heat, cover the pan with a lid and leave the rice to steam for a further 10–15 minutes. Fluff up the rice with a fork and serve hot, garnished with red chillies.

Serves four

450g/1lb/2¼ cups white long grain rice

30–45ml/2–3 tbsp vegetable or sesame oil

2–3 shallots, finely chopped

2 garlic cloves, finely chopped

400ml/14fl oz/1⅔ cups coconut milk

450ml/¾ pint/scant 2 cups water

10ml/2 tsp ground turmeric

3–4 fresh curry leaves

salt and ground black pepper

2 red chillies, seeded and finely sliced, to garnish

Per Portion Energy 487kcal/2035kJ; Protein 9.1g; Carbohydrate 96.5g, of which sugars 5.8g; Fat 6.7g, of which saturates 0.9g; Cholesterol 0mg; Calcium 70mg; Fibre 0.8g; Sodium 122mg.

Serves four

½ cucumber

30–45ml/2–3 tbsp vegetable or groundnut (peanut) oil, plus extra for shallow frying

4 shallots, finely chopped

4 garlic cloves, finely chopped

3–4 fresh red chillies, seeded and chopped

45ml/3 tbsp *kecap manis* (Indonesian sweet soy sauce)

15ml/1 tbsp tomato purée (paste)

350g/12oz/1¾ cups cooked long grain rice

4 eggs

Cook's tip If you don't have or can't find any *kecap manis*, you can substitute the same quantity of dark soy sauce mixed with a little sugar.

Indonesian fried rice
Nasi goreng

This dish of fried rice is one of Indonesia's national dishes. Generally made with leftover cooked grains, the fried rice is served with crispy shallots and chillies or it is tossed with shrimp or crabmeat, and chopped vegetables.

1 Peel the cucumber, cut in half lengthways and scoop out the seeds. Cut the flesh into thin sticks. Put aside.

2 In a wok, heat the 30–45ml/2–3 tbsp oil, stir in the shallots, garlic and chillies and fry until they begin to colour. Add the *kecap manis* and tomato purée and stir for 2 minutes until thick, to form a sauce. Toss in the cooked rice and cook for about 5 minutes until well flavoured and heated through.

3 Meanwhile, in a large frying pan, heat a thin layer of oil for frying and crack the eggs into it. Fry for 1–2 minutes until the whites are cooked but the yolks remain runny.

4 Spoon the rice into four deep bowls. Alternatively, use one bowl as a mould to invert each portion of rice on to individual plates then lift off the bowl to reveal the mound of rice beneath. Place a fried egg on top of each and garnish with the cucumber sticks.

Per Portion Energy 273kcal/1146kJ; Protein 9.9g; Carbohydrate 33g, of which sugars 4.7g; Fat 12.3g, of which saturates 2.5g; Cholesterol 190mg; Calcium 67mg; Fibre 1.1g; Sodium 884mg.

Fried rice with chorizo and fried eggs
Sinangag

This rice dish is a classic Filipino breakfast. To make a substantial meal to start the day, it is served at street stalls and cafés with fried dried fish, such as the crispy *danggit* from Cebu, fried eggs, pork jerky or the spicy sausage, *longaniza*, which can be substituted with the similar-tasting Spanish chorizo. This delicious recipe is a great way of using up leftover rice.

1 Heat 15–30ml/1–2 tbsp of the oil in a wok or heavy pan, stir in the garlic and fry until fragrant and golden brown. Toss in the rice, breaking up any lumps, and add the *patis*. Season the rice with salt to taste, if needed, and black pepper. Turn off the heat and cover the wok or pan to keep the rice warm.

2 In a heavy frying pan, heat 15ml/1 tbsp of the oil, add the sliced chorizo and fry until crispy on both sides. Drain the chorizo on kitchen paper.

3 Heat the remaining 15–30ml/1–2 tbsp oil in a separate frying pan and fry the eggs, sunny-side up for 1–2 minutes. Alternatively, fry the eggs over-easy, cooking them in the same way as sunny-side up then carefully turning the eggs over and frying for no more than 30 seconds until a film is set over the yolk without browning.

4 Spoon the rice on to individual serving plates. Alternatively, pack the rice into a cup or bowl and invert each portion of rice on to plates. Place the fried eggs on top of the rice and arrange the chorizo around the edge. Serve warm with the coconut vinegar.

Serves four

45–75ml/3–5 tbsp palm, groundnut (peanut) or vegetable oil

2–3 garlic cloves, crushed

450g/1lb cooked long grain rice

15–30ml/1–2 tbsp *patis* (fish sauce)

2 small, thin chorizo sausages, about 175g/6oz each, sliced diagonally

4 eggs

salt and ground black pepper

coconut vinegar, to serve

Cook's tip If you don't have any cooked, leftover long grain rice, cook 225g/8oz/ generous 1 cup rice, allow to cool and use in the same way as leftover rice.

Per Portion Energy 567kcal/2367kJ; Protein 17.7g; Carbohydrate 45.4g, of which sugars 2g; Fat 36.4g, of which saturates 11.6g; Cholesterol 225mg; Calcium 92mg; Fibre 0.6g; Sodium 1136mg.

Serves six

500g/1¼lb/2½ cups long grain rice

45–60ml/3–4 tbsp palm or groundnut (peanut) oil

12 chicken drumsticks and wings

2 onions, finely chopped

4 garlic cloves, finely chopped

40g/1½oz fresh root ginger, chopped

5ml/1 tsp paprika

30–45ml/2–3 tbsp tomato purée (paste)

2–3 bay leaves

1.2 litres/2 pints/5 cups chicken stock

15–30ml/1–2 tbsp *patis* (fish sauce)

400g/14oz can petit pois (baby peas), drained

12 prawns (shrimp) in their shells, cleaned and rinsed

12 medium clams, cleaned and rinsed

salt and ground black pepper

To serve

4 red chillies, seeded and quartered

kalamansi sauce

Filipino paella
Paella

Strikingly similar to Spanish paella and called by the same name, the Filipino version is packed with crabs, clams and prawns, although any shellfish can be used, and flavoured with ginger and bay leaves.

1 Put the rice in a sieve (strainer), rinse under cold running water until the water runs clear then drain. Heat the oil in a wok or wide, shallow heavy pan with a lid. Add the chicken drumsticks and wings and fry for about 5 minutes, until browned on both sides. Remove the chicken from the pan and put aside.

2 Add the onion, garlic and ginger to the pan and fry until fragrant and beginning to colour. Add the paprika, tomato purée, bay leaves and drained rice and toss in the chicken. Pour in the stock and bring to the boil. Add the *patis* and season with salt and lots of black pepper. Cover the pan and simmer gently for 15–20 minutes, until the rice and chicken are almost cooked.

3 Toss in the peas and add the prawns and clams, sitting them on top of the rice. Cover the pan again and cook for a further 10 minutes or until all the liquid has evaporated. Serve warm with kalamansi sauce and a bowl of chillies.

Cook's tip To make a perfect paella, it is essential to have a very wide, shallow, heavy pan with a lid.

Per Portion Energy 637kcal/2666kJ; Protein 54.4g; Carbohydrate 78.3g, of which sugars 4.6g; Fat 11.6g, of which saturates 2.1g; Cholesterol 266mg; Calcium 104mg; Fibre 3.8g; Sodium 628mg.

Filipino risotto with stir-fried liver
Aroz valenciana

It's not hard to guess the origins of this recipe! Made in a similar way to Italian risotto, the rice and pork are cooked in stock that is added gradually. This type of rice dish is usually served as a snack and much enjoyed at Christmas and Easter, when a vast number of pork-based dishes are cooked and shared with neighbours. If you cannot get hold of pig's liver, use lamb's liver, which is deliciously tender when cooked this way.

1 Put the rice in a sieve (strainer), rinse under cold running water until the water runs clear, then drain. Pour the stock into a pan and bring it to the boil. Make sure it is well seasoned, and then reduce the heat and leave to simmer.

2 Meanwhile, heat 30ml/2 tbsp of the oil in a wok or heavy pan, stir in the shallots, garlic, ginger and turmeric and fry until fragrant and beginning to colour. Add the raisins or currants and toss in the pork. Stir-fry for 2–3 minutes, until the pork is well browned. Toss in the rice, making sure that it is thoroughly mixed.

3 Gradually add ladlefuls of the hot stock to the rice and, stirring from time to time, cook over a medium heat until the liquid has been absorbed before adding another ladleful. When all the stock has been added, cover the pan and leave to cook gently, until almost all the liquid has been absorbed.

4 Meanwhile, toss the liver in the flour. Just before the rice is cooked, heat the remaining oil in a frying pan. Add the liver and stir-fry for 2–3 minutes. Season the liver with salt and pepper.

5 Tip the risotto into a warmed serving dish. Spoon the liver on top and scatter over the ground peanuts. Arrange the chopped eggs, spring onions and chillies around the dish and serve immediately with the coconut vinegar.

Serves three to four

225g/8oz/generous 1 cup sticky or glutinous rice

900ml/1½ pints pork or chicken stock

45–60ml/3–4 tbsp groundnut (peanut) or vegetable oil

3–4 shallots, finely chopped

3 garlic cloves, finely chopped

25g/1oz fresh root ginger, finely chopped

25g/1oz fresh turmeric, finely chopped

175g/6oz/¾ cup small raisins or currants

225g/8oz pork fillet, cut into thin bitesize strips

450g/1lb pig's liver, cut into bitesize strips

30–45ml/2–3 tbsp rice flour or plain (all-purpose) white flour

salt and ground black pepper

To serve

45–60ml/3–4 tbsp roasted, unsalted peanuts, crushed

2 hard-boiled eggs, quartered

2–3 spring onions (scallions), white parts only, sliced

2 red or green chillies, seeded and quartered lengthways

coconut vinegar

Per Portion Energy 756kcal/3167kJ; Protein 49.2g; Carbohydrate 87.7g, of which sugars 33.3g; Fat 23.3g, of which saturates 4.6g; Cholesterol 423mg; Calcium 74mg; Fibre 2.3g; Sodium 197mg.

Serves four to six

250g/9oz tofu block

corn or vegetable oil, for deep-frying

225g/8oz/1⅛ cup long grain jasmine rice

For the broth

15ml/1 tbsp palm or corn oil

2 garlic cloves, finely chopped

1–2 red or green chillies, seeded and finely chopped

1 lemon grass stalk, finely chopped

45ml/3 tbsp soy sauce

2 litres/3½ pints/8 cups chicken stock

450g/1lb fresh mung bean sprouts

For the noodles

500g/1¼lb fresh egg noodles or 225g/8oz dried egg noodles

30ml/2 tbsp palm or corn oil

4 shallots, finely sliced

2 garlic cloves, finely chopped

450g/1lb fresh shelled prawns (shrimp)

30ml/2 tbsp *kecap manis* (Indonesian sweet soy sauce)

ground black pepper

To serve

4–6 spring onions (scallions), finely sliced

chilli *sambal*

Cook's tip Although the tradition is to serve each ingredient in separate bowls, *nasi mi* is often served as a self-contained meal in a single dish at many street stalls.

Noodles and rice with tofu and beansprout broth
Nasi mi

The custom is to serve the noodles, rice, tofu, broth and *sambal* individually. Each person then spoons rice into a bowl, followed by the bean curd and *sambal*, then a ladleful of broth, with noodles eaten separately.

1 First prepare the tofu by cutting it into four rectangular pieces. Heat enough oil in a wok or heavy pan for deep-frying. Add the tofu pieces and fry for 2–3 minutes, until golden brown on both sides. Drain on kitchen paper. Cut the fried tofu into thin slices and pile them on a serving plate. Put aside.

2 Put the rice in a sieve (strainer), rinse under cold running water until the water runs clear, then drain. Transfer the rice to a pan and add about 600ml/1 pint/2½ cups water to cover the rice. Bring to the boil, reduce the heat then simmer gently for about 15 minutes, until all the water has been absorbed. Turn off the heat, cover the pan and leave to steam for a further 10–15 minutes.

3 Meanwhile, make the broth. Heat the oil in a heavy pan, stir in the garlic, chillies and lemon grass and fry until fragrant. Add 15ml/1 tbsp soy sauce and pour in the chicken stock. Bring to the boil, reduce the heat and simmer for 10–15 minutes.

4 Meanwhile, if using dried noodles, soak in warm water for 5 minutes until softened. Season the broth with the remaining soy sauce and pepper and stir in the mung bean sprouts. Turn off the heat and keep warm.

5 Finally, prepare the noodles. Heat the oil in a wok, stir in the shallots and garlic and fry until they begin to colour. Toss in the prawns and cook for 2 minutes, then stir in the *kecap manis* with 15–30ml/1–2 tbsp water. Add the noodles, season and toss well.

6 Tip the rice and noodles on to warmed serving dishes and serve with the tofu, a bowl of spring onions, chilli *sambal* and a bowl of the steaming hot broth, so that everyone can help themselves.

Per Portion Energy 690kcal/2900kJ; Protein 32.6g; Carbohydrate 97g, of which sugars 5.9g; Fat 20.7g, of which saturates 3.6g; Cholesterol 171mg; Calcium 328mg; Fibre 4.2g; Sodium 833mg.

Indonesian stir-fried noodles
Bakmie goreng

Serves four

450g/1lb fresh egg noodles

15–30ml/1–2 tbsp palm, groundnut (peanut) or corn oil, plus extra for shallow frying

2 shallots, finely chopped

2–3 spring onions (scallions), finely chopped

2–3 garlic cloves, crushed

3–4 Thai chillies, seeded and finely chopped

15ml/1 tbsp *terasi* (Indonesian shrimp paste)

15ml/1 tbsp tomato purée (paste)

15–30ml/1–2 tbsp *kecap manis* (Indonesian sweet soy sauce)

4 eggs

salt

To garnish

15ml/1 tbsp palm or corn oil

3–4 shallots, finely sliced

Originally from China, stir-fried noodles have become as popular as stir-fried rice at street stalls throughout Indonesia, and are just as varied.

1 First prepare the garnish. Heat the oil in a heavy pan, stir in the shallots and fry until deep golden brown. Drain on kitchen paper and put aside.

2 Fill a deep pan with water and bring it to the boil. Drop in the egg noodles, untangling them with chopsticks, and cook for about 3 minutes until tender but still firm to the bite. Drain and refresh under running cold water.

3 Heat the oil in a wok or large, heavy frying pan and fry the shallots, spring onions, garlic and chillies until fragrant. Add the *terasi* and cook until the mixture darkens.

4 Toss the noodles into the pan, making sure that they are thoroughly coated in the mixture. Add the tomato purée and *kecap manis*, toss thoroughly, and cook for 2–3 minutes. Season the noodles with salt to taste. Divide the noodles between four warmed bowls and keep warm.

5 Heat a thin layer of oil in a large, heavy frying pan, and crack the eggs into it. Fry for 1–2 minutes until the whites are cooked but the yolks remain runny. Place on the noodles and serve immediately with the fried shallots sprinkled over the top.

Per Portion Energy 549kcal/2317kJ; Protein 20.5g; Carbohydrate 82.9g, of which sugars 3.9g; Fat 17.6g, of which saturates 4.5g; Cholesterol 224mg; Calcium 68mg; Fibre 3.7g; Sodium 549mg.

Celebration noodles
Pancit palabok

Reserved mainly for special occasions and celebrations, such as birthdays and weddings, this is one of the national dishes of the Philippines. Packed with ingredients and topped with chopped egg, these traditional stir-fried noodles vary from region to region but are every Filipino cook's pride and joy.

1 Heat 15ml/1 tbsp oil in a wok or a large, heavy frying pan, stir in the onion and garlic and fry until fragrant and beginning to colour. Toss in the pork and shrimp and stir-fry for 2 minutes, then tip the mixture on to a plate.

2 Return the wok to the heat, add the remaining oil then stir in the carrots and cabbage and stir-fry for 2–3 minutes. Tip the vegetables on to the plate with the pork and shrimp.

3 Pour the stock, soy sauce and sugar into the wok and stir until the sugar has dissolved. Add the noodles, untangling them with chopsticks, and cook for about 3 minutes, until tender but still firm to the bite. Toss in the pork, shrimp, cabbage and carrots, making sure that they are thoroughly mixed.

4 Tip the noodles on to a warmed serving dish and scatter the chopped eggs over the top. Serve immediately with the lime wedges to squeeze over them.

Serves four

30ml/2 tbsp palm or coconut oil

1 large onion, finely chopped

2–3 garlic cloves, finely chopped

250g/9oz pork loin, cut into thin strips

250g/9oz fresh shelled shrimp

2 carrots, cut into matchsticks

½ small green cabbage, finely shredded

about 250ml/8fl oz/1 cup pork or chicken stock

50ml/2fl oz/¼ cup soy sauce

15ml/1 tbsp palm sugar

450g/1lb fresh egg noodles

2 hard-boiled eggs, finely chopped

1 lime, quartered

Cook's tip Fresh egg noodles are available in Chinese and South-east Asian stores.

Per Portion Energy 728kcal/3069kJ; Protein 43.6g; Carbohydrate 98g, of which sugars 16.9g; Fat 20.8g, of which saturates 5g; Cholesterol 290mg; Calcium 159mg; Fibre 6.3g; Sodium 1303mg.

Indonesian deep-fried spring rolls
Lumpia goreng

Made with a crêpe-style batter using rice flour, these Indonesian spring rolls are packed with vegetables and strips of chicken and then dipped in *kecap manis*, which is often spiked with chillies. Extra chillies, seeded and thinly sliced, can be served on the side, if you like.

Serves three to four

15–30ml/1–2 tbsp palm or corn oil

2–3 garlic cloves, finely chopped

225g/8oz chicken breast fillets, cut into fine strips

225g/8oz fresh shrimp, shelled

2 leeks, cut into matchsticks

2 carrots, cut into matchsticks

½ green cabbage, finely shredded

175g/6oz fresh beansprouts

30ml/2 tbsp *patis* (fish sauce)

30ml/2 tbsp *kecap manis* (Indonesian sweet soy sauce)

1 egg, lightly beaten

corn or vegetable oil, for deep-frying

4 red or green Thai chillies, seeded and finely sliced, to serve

For the spring roll wrappers

115g/4oz/1 cup plus 30ml/2 tbsp rice flour

30ml/2 tbsp tapioca flour or cornflour (cornstarch)

2 eggs, beaten

15ml/1 tbsp palm or coconut oil

about 400ml/14fl oz/scant 2 cups water

salt

corn or vegetable oil, for frying

For the dipping sauce

about 200ml/7fl oz/scant 1 cup *kecap manis* (Indonesian sweet soy sauce)

1 red Thai chilli, seeded and chopped

1 First make the spring roll wrappers. Sift the rice flour and tapioca flour or cornflour into a bowl. Make a well in the centre, add the beaten eggs and oil into the well and gradually pour in the water, beating all the time until a smooth batter is formed. Season with salt and leave the batter to rest for 30 minutes.

2 Heat a small, heavy, non-stick frying pan and, using a piece of kitchen paper, wipe a little oil for frying all over the surface. Using a small cup or ladle, add a little of the batter to the pan, tilting it to spread the batter evenly over the base. There should be enough batter to make 12 wrappers. Reduce the heat and cook gently on one side, until the batter is lightly browned and lifts at the edges. Lift the wrapper on to a plate and keep fresh under a clean, damp dish towel. Repeat with the remaining batter.

3 To prepare the filling, heat 15ml/1 tbsp oil in a wok or large, heavy frying pan, stir in the garlic and fry until fragrant. Add the chicken and shrimp and stir-fry for 2–3 minutes, until just cooked. Tip on to a plate and return the wok to the heat.

4 Add the remaining oil to the wok, add the leeks, carrots, and cabbage and stir-fry for 2–3 minutes. Toss in the beansprouts and stir-fry for further 1–2 minutes. Add the chicken, shrimp, *patis* and *kecap manis* and toss until all the ingredients are thoroughly combined and coated in the sauce. Tip the mixture on to a plate and leave to cool.

5 To fill the spring rolls, place a wrapper on a flat surface and drop a heaped spoonful of the filling on the side nearest to you. Spread the filling to form a log, then roll the edge nearest to you over the mixture, tuck in the sides and continue rolling the wrapper away from you. When you get to the far side, moisten it with a little of the beaten egg to seal the seam. Repeat to make 12 spring rolls.

6 Before frying the spring rolls, quickly prepare the dipping sauce. Pour the *kecap manis* into a serving bowl, stir in the chopped chilli, and place the bowl next to the serving dish for the spring rolls or in the middle of it.

7 In a wok or heavy pan, heat enough oil for deep-frying. Carefully lower one or two spring rolls at a time into the pan and sizzle gently for 3–4 minutes, until golden brown and crisp. Using a slotted spoon, remove from the pan and drain on kitchen paper. Transfer to the serving dish and serve immediately, with the dipping sauce and the sliced chillies on the side.

Per Portion Energy 585kcal/2446kJ; Protein 35.4g; Carbohydrate 43.5g, of which sugars 7.2g; Fat 31.2g, of which saturates 4.5g; Cholesterol 292mg; Calcium 170mg; Fibre 5.1g; Sodium 744mg.

Fresh spring rolls with palm heart
Lumpia ubod

Prepared for special occasions, *lumpia ubod* is quite a treat as it contains the tender heart of a three- to five-year-old palm tree. Coconut palm trees grow all over the Philippines and there are some that are grown specifically for the heart, although all parts of the palm tree are used.

1 First make the spring roll wrappers. Sift the flour, tapioca flour or cornflour and salt into a bowl. Gradually pour in the water and whisk until a smooth batter is formed. Leave to rest for 30 minutes.

2 Heat a non-stick pancake or crêpe pan and, using a piece of kitchen paper, wipe a little oil for frying all over the surface. Ladle a little of the batter into the pan, tilting it to spread the batter evenly over the base. In total there should be enough batter to make 12 wrappers. Cook over a medium-low heat, on one side only, until the batter sets, is pale in colour, begins to bubble up in the middle and loosens at the edges. Carefully transfer the wrapper to a plate. Repeat with the remaining batter. Put aside.

3 To prepare the filling, cut the carrots into 5cm/2in long matchsticks and put aside. Cut off the green stems of the spring onions, halve lengthways and put aside. Cut the white stems into 5cm/2in lengths and then quarter each piece lengthways. Put aside. Blanch the palm hearts in a pan of boiling water for 2–3 minutes, refresh under cold running water then cut into 5cm/2in strips. Put aside.

4 Cut the tofu into three rectangular pieces. Heat 15–30ml/1–2 tbsp oil in a wok or heavy frying pan, add the tofu pieces and fry until golden brown on both sides. Drain on kitchen paper, then cut each piece into thin strips and put aside.

5 Add the garlic to the wok and fry until fragrant. Toss in the carrots and stir-fry for 2–3 minutes. Add the white parts of the spring onions and the prawns and fry until they turn opaque. Add the palm hearts and tofu strips, followed by the soy sauce and sugar. Season the filling to taste and tip the mixture on to a plate to cool.

6 Place a spring roll wrapper on a flat surface and position a lettuce leaf on it, making sure the frilly edge overlaps the wrapper on the side furthest away from you. Spoon some of the mixture into the middle of the leaf, making sure the strips of carrot, tofu and palm heart overlap the wrapper by the frilly edge of the lettuce. Fold the edge nearest to you over the filling and fold in the sides to form a bundle with the palm heart, carrot, tofu and frill of lettuce poking out of the top.

7 Using the reserved green spring onions, tie the bundle with a green ribbon and place it on a serving dish. Repeat with the remaining wrappers and filling to make 12 spring rolls. Serve with coconut vinegar for dipping.

Serves three to four

1–2 carrots

6 spring onions (scallions)

400g/14oz can coconut palm heart, drained

225g/8oz tofu, rinsed

30–45ml/2–3 tbsp coconut or groundnut (peanut) oil

2 garlic cloves, finely chopped

12 fresh prawns (shrimp), shelled and deveined

30–45ml/2–3 tbsp light soy sauce

10ml/2 tsp sugar

salt and ground black pepper

coconut vinegar, to serve

For the spring roll wrappers

115g/4oz/1 cup plain (all-purpose) white flour

15ml/1 tbsp tapioca flour or cornflour (cornstarch)

pinch of salt

400ml/14fl oz/1⅔ cups water

corn oil, for frying

Per Portion Energy 307kcal/1289kJ; Protein 19.5g; Carbohydrate 32.8g, of which sugars 7g; Fat 11.7g, of which saturates 1.4g; Cholesterol 122mg; Calcium 433mg; Fibre 2.8g; Sodium 797mg.

Vegetables and salads

Vegetables and salads

Indonesia and the Philippines both have an abundance of fruit and vegetables, including both indigenous varieties and those imported by early settlers. Whether it's in a large city market, a makeshift stall, a small garden or a basket by the side of a rural road, the choice is magnificent, and it is hardly surprising that both cuisines make full use of the produce on offer to create delectable savoury and sweet dishes.

Among the selection on offer there are some indigenous vegetables, such as the yam, taro, cassava and water spinach (*kangkung*), but there are also many vegetables that were brought in from elsewhere during the long history of trade and colonization of the two nations, such as aubergines (eggplants) from India and corn, sweet potatoes and tomatoes from the New World.

The bustling indoor and open-air markets are generally vivid and lively, and are usually filled with huge baskets of red chillies, bouquets of galangal, bright purple aubergines, coils of long green snake beans (yardlong beans), bunches of intensely yellow bananas still on the branch, huge pumpkins and hairy coconuts.

The most commonly used vegetable of all in Indonesian cooking is the shallot (*bawang merah*). Pounded with garlic and other flavourings, shallots are at the foundation of every meal in the spice paste. Stir-fried they add flavour to rice and noodle dishes and deep-fried they are used to garnish many dishes. The larger onion tends to be commonly used and is called *bawang Bombay*, which gives us a clue as to where it probably originated.

Soya beans also feature widely in Indonesian cuisine, mainly in the form of tofu, which is called *tahu*, or as *tempe*, which are fermented bean cakes. High in protein and with a rich, nutty flavour, tempeh is a popular and very versatile snack, which can be cooked in stock, deep-fried or stir-fried in a sweet sauce. Sumedang in West Java is said to have the best-tasting fried tofu (*tahu goring*) in Indonesia. Tofu stuffed with beansprouts (*tahu isi*) is another speciality of the region.

The home-grown produce of Indonesia and the Philippines is very similar. How they use it may differ, but with a similar climate, regular rainfall and fertile volcanic soil, both regions

Above, from left to right *Aubergines (eggplants) in chilli sauce* (terong belado)*; fresh okra; salad in tangy dressing* (rujak).

produce the nutritious, leafy water spinach (called *kangkung* in both Indonesia and the Philippines), which grows on wet and dry ground, and is packed with iron and vitamins. For best results, water spinach is simply stir-fried with garlic and chillies and a little soy sauce.

Various types of green beans and cabbages, asparagus, carrots, leeks and beansprouts are also grown in both regions The wide-leafed cassava plant (*singkong*), grows widely throughout the region and every part of the tuber is used. It is very versatile and can be pounded to a powder, deep-fried, roasted, boiled, added to stews and fermented to make *tape*, a sweet and delicious Balinese dessert that can be made by fermenting cooked cassava or sticky rice.

Taro, corn and sago palms are also cultivated as staples in the areas of the two countries where rice does not grow well. Taro is grown primarily for its carbohydrate-rich corm, which must be cooked, although the vitamin- and mineral-rich leaves and flowers can also be eaten. Corn has many uses, including being used to make spicy patties, or served simply roasted. Sago is the staple of Nusa Tenggara, where the starchy trunk of the palm is stripped, ground, washed and strained before being used to make thick porridge.

In Irian Jaya, the western part of New Guinea, the sweet potato is king of vegetables. This staple, which was originally a New World contribution to South-east Asia, has been so absorbed into the culinary culture of the region, you would think it was an indigenous plant, especially as the Dani grow

about sixty varieties of the tuber. Varieties of regular potatoes are also widely grown in both Indonesia and the Philippines. Generally, they are fried or mashed to form fritters.

In West Java, the Sundanese are reputed to live off their greens, particularly various types of green bean. The textured chilli salad, *karedok* (raw vegetable and coconut salad in a lime dressing), made with snake beans (yardlong beans), cucumber and beansprouts, is a Sundanese speciality.

As with other parts of South-east Asia, unripe fruits are often treated as vegetables. Hence, the noble green papaya is sliced finely and tossed in salads and soups. Light and crunchy, with a hint of bitterness, it is also often dressed in lime juice and served with hot, spicy dishes. Green mango, which has a similar texture and sourness to green papaya, is used in the same fashion.

There are numerous varieties of banana, some of which are firmer and more akin to their cousin the plantain. Both are frequently sliced and deep-fried as a savoury snack or added to stews. The purple bud that hangs at the end of a clump of bananas is also used as a vegetable. The leaves and tiny buds are removed to reveal a delicate, creamy white centre which is used in salads and spring rolls.

Eggs often go hand in hand with vegetables, particularly in stir-fried noodle dishes and omelettes. They also feature in the Javanese jackfruit curry, *gudeg*, and the Indonesian classic *gado gado* (steamed vegetables and fruit with peanut sauce), and are often hard-boiled, chopped and sprinkled over salads.

Above, from left to right *Snake bean (yardlong bean) stew* (linagang sitaw)*; beansprouts; red mustard leaf salad* (mostasa salada).

Aubergines in a chilli sauce
Terong belado

This dish is a great Indonesian favourite, both in the home and at the street stall. You can make it with large aubergines, cut in half and baked, or with small ones, butterflied. The dip is served in the aubergines' skin.

1 Preheat oven to 180°C/350°F/Gas 4. Put the prepared aubergines on a baking tray and brush with 30ml/2 tbsp of the coconut oil. Bake in the oven for 40 minutes, until they are soft and tender.

2 Using a mortar and pestle, grind the shallots, garlic, ginger and chillies to a paste. Heat the remaining 15ml/1 tbsp of oil in a wok and stir in the spice paste and cook for 1–2 minutes. Add the tomatoes and sugar and cook for 3–4 minutes, then stir in the lime juice and a little salt to taste.

3 Put the baked aubergines on to a serving dish and press down the flesh to form a dip, using the back of a wooden spoon. Spoon the sauce into the dip and over the aubergines. Garnish with the chopped coriander and serve warm or at room temperature.

Serves four

2 large aubergines (eggplants), cut in half lengthways, or 4 small auberines, butterflied

45–60ml/3–4 tbsp coconut oil

4 shallots, finely chopped

4 garlic cloves, finely chopped

25g/1oz fresh root ginger, finely chopped

3–4 red chillies, seeded and finely chopped

400g/14oz can tomatoes, drained

5–10ml/1–2 tsp palm sugar

juice of 2 limes

salt

1 small bunch fresh coriander (cilantro), finely chopped, to garnish

Per Portion Energy 100kcal/419kJ; Protein 2.1g; Carbohydrate 9.4g, of which sugars 8.8g; Fat 6.4g, of which saturates 0.9g; Cholesterol 0mg; Calcium 42mg; Fibre 3.7g; Sodium 15mg.

Aubergine, bitter melon and okra stew with bagnet
Pinakbet

This classic Filipino dish is flavoured with the much-loved *bagoong*, the fermented anchovy sauce, which is available in South-east Asian and Filipino supermarkets. The *bagnet* lends a rich meaty flavour to this stew, which compliments the fermented fish, resulting in a tasty main course dish.

Serves four to six

225g/8oz okra

juice of 1 lime

1 bitter melon

15–30ml/1–2 tbsp palm or corn oil

1–3 garlic cloves, crushed

25g/1oz fresh root ginger, grated

4 shallots, thickly sliced

350g/12oz *bagnet* (crispy fried pork belly)

15–30ml/1–2 tbsp *bagoong* or 15ml/1 tbsp shrimp paste

400g/14oz can plum tomatoes

250ml/8fl oz/1 cup pork or chicken stock

1 aubergine (eggplant), cut into bitesize wedges, or 2–3 Thai aubergines, quartered

salt and ground black pepper

cooked rice, to serve

1 Put the okra in a large bowl, add the lime juice, toss together and leave to marinate for 30 minutes. Cut the melon in half lengthways, remove the core then cut the flesh into bitesize chunks. Put aside.

2 Meanwhile, heat the oil in a wok or a large, heavy pan, stir in the garlic and ginger and fry until fragrant. Add the shallots and fry for about 5 minutes until golden brown. Stir in the *bagnet* and fry for 1 minute, then add the *bagoong*, tomatoes and stock. Bring to the boil, reduce the heat and simmer for about 10 minutes.

3 Drain the aubergine, bitter melon and okra and add to the pan and cook for a further 10–15 minutes until the vegetables are tender but not too soft. Season the stew with salt and pepper to taste and serve with rice.

Cook's tip If you can't find *bagoong*, you could substitute it with a Filipino, Indonesian or Thai shrimp paste.

Per Portion Energy 323kcal/1340kJ; Protein 16.1g; Carbohydrate 9.4g, of which sugars 8.9g; Fat 24.8g, of which saturates 8.2g; Cholesterol 74mg; Calcium 118mg; Fibre 3.3g; Sodium 200mg.

Bicolano snake bean stew
Linagang sitaw

Known as Bicol, the southern Luzon peninsula in the Philippines is renowned for its fiery food, laced with hot chillies and coconut milk. In typical Bicolano style, this rich, pungent dish is hot and, believe it or not, it is served with extra chillies to chew on!

1 Heat the oil in a wok or large, heavy frying pan that has a lid. Stir in the onion, garlic, ginger, lemon grass and chillies and fry until fragrant and beginning to colour. Add the *bagoong* or shrimp paste, tamarind paste and sugar and stir in the coconut milk and lime leaves.

2 Bring the mixture to the boil, reduce the heat and toss in the whole snake beans. Partially cover the pan and cook the beans gently for 6–8 minutes until tender. Season the stew with salt and pepper to taste and sprinkle with chopped coriander to garnish. Serve with rice and extra chillies to chew on.

Cook's tip If preferred, you can reduce the quantity of chillies used in the recipe to suit your taste buds and you do not have to serve the stew with extra chillies if you don't want to.

Serves three to four

30–45ml/2–3 tbsp coconut or groundnut oil

1 onion, finely chopped

2–3 garlic cloves, finely chopped

40g/1½oz fresh root ginger, finely chopped

1 lemon grass stalk, finely chopped

4–5 red chillies, seeded and finely chopped

15–30ml/1–2 tbsp *bagoong* or 15ml/1 tbsp shrimp paste

15–30ml/1–2 tbsp tamarind paste

15–30ml/1–2 tbsp palm sugar

2 x 400g/14oz cans unsweetened coconut milk

4 kaffir lime leaves

500g/1¼lb snake beans (yardlong beans)

salt and ground black pepper

1 bunch of fresh coriander (cilantro) leaves, roughly chopped, to garnish

To serve

cooked rice

raw chillies

Per Portion Energy 200kcal/840kJ; Protein 5.5g; Carbohydrate 24.4g, of which sugars 22.9g; Fat 9.7g, of which saturates 1.5g; Cholesterol 19mg; Calcium 158mg; Fibre 3.4g; Sodium 384mg.

Serves four

1 small, firm pineapple

155–30ml/1–2 tbsp palm or coconut oil

4–6 shallots, finely chopped

2 garlic cloves, finely chopped

1 red chilli, seeded and finely chopped

15ml/1 tbsp palm sugar

400ml/14fl oz/1⅔ cups coconut milk

salt and ground black pepper

1 small bunch fresh coriander (cilantro) leaves, finely chopped, to garnish

For the spice paste

4 cloves

4 cardamom pods

1 small cinnamon stick

5ml/1 tsp coriander seeds

2.5ml/½ tsp cumin seeds

5–10ml/1–2 tsp water

Pineapple and coconut curry
Pacari

This sweet and spicy curry from the Maluku spice islands benefits from being made the day before eating, enabling the flavours to mingle longer. In Indonesia it is often eaten at room temperature, but it is also delicious hot.

1 First make the spice paste. Using a mortar and pestle or electric spice grinder, grind all the spices together to a powder. In a small bowl mix the spice powder with the water to make a paste. Put aside.

2 Remove the skin from the pineapple then cut the flesh lengthways into quarters and remove the core. Cut each quarter widthways into chunky slices and put aside.

3 Heat the oil in a wok or large, heavy frying pan, stir in the shallots, garlic and chilli and stir-fry until fragrant and beginning to colour. Stir in the spice paste and fry for 1 minute. Toss in the pineapple, making sure the slices are coated in the spicy mixture.

4 Stir the sugar into the coconut milk and pour into the wok. Stir and bring to the boil. Reduce the heat and simmer for 3–4 minutes to thicken the sauce, but do not allow the pineapple to become too soft. Season with salt and pepper to taste.

5 Tip the curry into a warmed serving dish and sprinkle with the chopped coriander to garnish. Serve hot or at room temperature.

Per Portion Energy 135kcal/573kJ; Protein 1.6g; Carbohydrate 25.4g, of which sugars 23.6g; Fat 3.8g, of which saturates 0.5g; Cholesterol 0mg; Calcium 87mg; Fibre 2.9g; Sodium 131mg.

Steamed vegetables and fruit with peanut sauce
Gado Gado

This classic Indonesian dish of vegetables in a peanut sauce is enjoyed throughout the islands, which means there are many variations as each region will incorporate their local vegetables and fruit. Served at room temperature with a bowl of rice, this dish could be an appetizer or a meal on its own.

1 First make the peanut sauce. Heat the oil in a wok or heavy pan, stir in the shallots, garlic and chillies and fry until fragrant and beginning to colour. Add the peanuts, galangal, *terasi* and palm sugar and fry for about 4 minutes, until the peanuts begin to darken and ooze a little oil.

2 Pour the coconut milk, lime juice and *kecap manis* into the pan and bring to the boil. Reduce the heat and simmer gently for 15–20 minutes, until the sauce has reduced a little and thickened. Leave to cool.

3 Cut the tofu into four rectangular pieces. Heat enough oil in a wok for deep-frying, add the tofu pieces and fry until golden brown. Using a slotted spoon, remove from the pan and drain on kitchen paper. Cut the tofu into slices and put aside.

4 Heat 15–30ml/1–2 tbsp of the oil in a small, heavy pan, add the shallots and fry until deep golden in colour. Drain on kitchen paper and put aside.

5 Fill a large pan a third of the way up with water and place a steaming basket over it. Bring the water to the boil and put the carrots and snake beans in the steaming basket. Put the lid on, reduce the heat, and steam for 3–4 minutes. Add the *kangkung* for a minute, then drain the vegetables and refresh under cold running water.

6 Put the vegetables in a large bowl. Add the mango, pineapple and bean sprouts and pour in half the peanut sauce. Toss well and tip on to a serving dish. Arrange the egg quarters and tofu slices around the edge and drizzle the remaining peanut sauce over the top. Sprinkle with the reserved fried shallots and chopped coriander to garnish.

Serves four to six

500g/1¼lb tofu block

corn oil, for deep frying

4 shallots, finely sliced

3 carrots, sliced diagonally

about 12 snake beans (yardlong beans), cut into bitesize pieces

225g/8oz *kangkung* (water spinach), washed and thinly sliced

1 firm mango, cut into bitesize chunks

½ pineapple, cut into bitesize chunks

225g/8oz mung bean sprouts

2–3 hard-boiled eggs, quartered

salt

1 small bunch fresh coriander (cilantro) leaves, roughly chopped, to garnish

For the peanut sauce

30ml/2 tbsp coconut or groundnut (peanut) oil

3 shallots, finely chopped

3 garlic cloves, finely chopped

3–4 red chillies, seeded and finely chopped

175g/6oz/1 cup unsalted roasted peanuts, finely ground

15g/½oz galangal or fresh root ginger, finely chopped

5–10ml/1–2 tsp *terasi* (Indonesian shrimp paste)

15ml/1 tbsp palm sugar

600ml/1 pint/2½ cups coconut milk

juice of 1 lime

30ml/2 tbsp *kecap manis* (Indonesian sweet soy sauce)

Cook's tip Other ingredients commonly used for *gado gado* include shredded cabbage, sweet potato, turnip, papaya and star fruit (carambola).

Per Portion Energy 449kcal/1873kJ; Protein 22.2g; Carbohydrate 24.5g, of which sugars 20.7g; Fat 30g, of which saturates 5.1g; Cholesterol 108mg; Calcium 611mg; Fibre 5.1g; Sodium 675mg.

Raw vegetable and coconut salad in a lime dressing
Karedok

This Indonesian salad is typical of the type of dish that is served as a snack with rice on a banana leaf, or with grilled or fried fish and meat. Street stalls often prepare a simple salad of this kind to accompany the main dish. Crunchy and easy to eat with the fingers, the salad varies according to which vegetables are in season. Serve it as an accompaniment to meat, poultry or fish along with bowls of rice.

Serves four to six

225g/8oz snake beans (yardlong beans), cut into bitesize pieces

3–4 tomatoes, skinned, seeded and cut into bitesize chunks

4–6 spring onions (scallions), sliced

225g/8oz beansprouts

½ fresh coconut, grated

For the dressing

1–2 red or green chillies, seeded and chopped

2 garlic cloves, chopped

25g/1oz galangal or fresh root ginger, grated

5–10ml/1–2 tsp *terasi* (shrimp paste)

juice of 2–3 limes

salt and ground black pepper

1 To make the dressing, using a mortar and pestle, grind the chillies, garlic or galangal to a paste. Add the *terasi* and juice of 2 limes. If the limes are not juicy, then squeeze the juice of the extra lime and add to the dressing or add a little water, so that it is of pouring consistency. Season the dressing with salt and pepper to taste.

2 Put the snake beans, tomatoes, spring onions, beansprouts and grated coconut into a large bowl. Using your fingers or two spoons, mix the ingredients together, then toss in the dressing. Serve as an accompaniment to meat, poultry or fish and bowls of rice.

Per Portion Energy 141kcal/584kJ; Protein 4.5g; Carbohydrate 6.4g, of which sugars 5.1g; Fat 11g, of which saturates 9.1g; Cholesterol 8mg; Calcium 54mg; Fibre 4.6g; Sodium 86mg.

Green papaya salad
Atsarang papaya

Throughout South-east Asia, unripe green mangoes and papayas are used for salads. Their tart, crunchy flesh complements spicy grilled or stir-fried dishes beautifully. This Filipino version is sweet and sour, achieving the desired balance for grilled or deep-fried pork and chicken.

1 Put the papaya, shallots, chillies, sultanas or raisins, garlic and ginger into a bowl. In a separate small bowl, mix together the coconut vinegar and sugar until the sugar has dissolved.

2 Pour the sweet vinegar over the salad and toss well together. Leave the salad to marinate for at least 1 hour or, for the best flavour, in the refrigerator overnight to allow the flavours to mingle. Serve garnished with coriander leaves.

Serves four

2 green papayas, seeded and grated

4 shallots, finely sliced

1–2 red chillies, seeded, halved lengthways and finely sliced

150g/5oz/1 cup plump sultanas (golden raisins) or raisins

2 garlic cloves, crushed

25g/1oz fresh root ginger, grated

45–60ml/3–4 tbsp coconut or cane vinegar

50g/2oz palm sugar

1 small bunch of coriander (cilantro)

Variation Use green mango or grated carrots, or you can combine the papaya with carrots for their vibrant colours.

Per Portion Energy 232kcal/988kJ; Protein 2.5g; Carbohydrate 58.3g, of which sugars 57.6g; Fat 0.4g, of which saturates 0g; Cholesterol 0mg; Calcium 81mg; Fibre 5.5g; Sodium 19mg.

Refreshing fruit salad in a tangy dressing
Rujak

Entrenched in the Indonesian culinary culture, *rujak* appears in its many guises – as a snack, as a salad to accompany fried and grilled dishes, or as a festive dish. In Java, it is traditionally served before the birth of the first child. In the 19th century, Javanese settlers introduced it to Malaysia, where it has been adapted by the Chinese, Indian and Malays to suit their tastes. Designed to be flexible, this refreshing salad, tossed in a pungent and tangy dressing, can include any choice of fruit and vegetables that you like.

Serves four to six

1 green mango, finely sliced

1 ripe, firm papaya, finely sliced

1–2 star fruit (carambola), finely sliced

½ pineapple, finely sliced and cut into bitesize pieces

½ pomelo, segmented

1 small cucumber, roughly peeled, deseeded, and finely sliced

1 yam bean, finely sliced

a handful of beansprouts

For the sauce

10ml/2 tsp *terasi* (shrimp paste)

225g/8oz roasted peanuts

4 garlic cloves, chopped

2–4 red chillies, seeded and chopped

15ml/1 tbsp tamarind paste

30ml/2 tbsp palm sugar

salt

1 To make the sauce, dry-roast the *terasi* in a small, heavy frying pan until browned and emitting a toasted, pungent aroma.

2 Using a mortar and pestle or an electric blender, pound the peanuts, garlic and chillies to a coarse paste. Beat in the dry-fried *terasi*, tamarind paste and sugar. Add enough water to make a thick, pouring sauce then stir until the sugar has dissolved. Season the sauce with salt to taste.

3 Put all the fruit and vegetables, except the beansprouts, into a large bowl. Pour in some of the sauce and toss gently together. Leave the salad to stand for 30 minutes.

4 Turn the salad into a serving dish. Scatter the beansprouts over the top and serve with the remaining sauce drizzled on top.

Cook's tip Like *gado gado*, the vegetables and fruit used in this refreshing salad can be interchanged with carrots, turnip, jackfruit and sweet potato.

Per Portion Energy 321kcal/1344kJ; Protein 12.3g; Carbohydrate 30g, of which sugars 27.2g; Fat 17.7g, of which saturates 3.3g; Cholesterol 8mg; Calcium 91mg; Fibre 6.2g; Sodium 81mg.

Seaweed salad with green mango
Gulamen salada

In Japan, seaweed is consumed widely in its various forms but this tradition has not filtered through the rest of South-east Asia to the same degree. In the Philippines though, various types of seaweed are enjoyed in salads and the occasional stir-fry. Serve this salad as an appetizer or as an accompaniment to grilled meats and fish.

1 Bring a large pan of water to the boil, drop in the seaweed, remove from the heat and leave to soak for 15 minutes. Drain and refresh under cold running water. Using your hands, squeeze the seaweed dry.

2 Put the seaweed, mango, tomatoes, spring onions and ginger into a large bowl. In a separate bowl, mix together the coconut vinegar, chilli oil and sugar until the sugar has dissolved. Pour the dressing over the salad, toss well together and season with salt and pepper to taste. Serve as an appetizer or with grilled (broiled) meat or fish.

Cook's tip Fresh and dried seaweeds are available in Chinese and South-east Asian supermarkets, but some dried varieties are available in health food stores. For this recipe, you need the fine thread seaweed available in Chinese stores.

Serves four

50g/2oz fine thread seaweed, reconstituted in water, or 225g/8oz fresh seaweed, cut into strips

1 green mango, grated

2–3 ripe tomatoes, skinned, seeded and chopped

4–6 spring onions (scallions), white parts only, sliced

25g/1oz fresh root ginger, grated

45ml/3 tbsp coconut or cane vinegar

10ml/2 tsp chilli oil

15ml/1 tbsp sugar

salt and ground black pepper

Per Portion Energy 75kcal/315kJ; Protein 2.4g; Carbohydrate 12g, of which sugars 11.8g; Fat 2.2g, of which saturates 0.3g; Cholesterol 0mg; Calcium 110mg; Fibre 2.8g; Sodium 85mg.

Red mustard leaf salad
Mostasa salada

Leafy greens, such as water spinach, Chinese cabbages and the leaves of various plants are rarely served as a salad in South-east Asia; instead they are stir–fried and served with rice to balance a meal. However, the Filipinos enjoy red mustard leaves and the leaves of the sweet potato plant in salads, to accompany fried fish, or roasted or grilled meat.

Serves four

700g/1lb 9oz mustard leaves

3 ripe tomatoes, skinned, seeded and chopped

4–6 spring onions (scallions), chopped

30–45ml/2–3 tbsp coconut or cane vinegar

salt and ground back pepper

1 Rinse the mustard leaves very well in cold water then drain. Put the leaves in a large bowl and sprinkle with salt. Rub the salt into the leaves, crunching and squeezing them with your fingers, to soften them and begin to draw out their juices. Leave to stand for 30 minutes to draw out the bitter juices.

2 Lift up the leaves in your hands and squeeze them tightly to drain off the juice. Rinse the leaves again in cold water and drain well.

3 Put the leaves in a salad bowl and add the tomatoes and spring onions. Add the vinegar and season with a little salt, if required, and pepper and toss well together. Serve as a appetizer, with fried fish, or with roasted or grilled (broiled) meat.

Cook's tip Red mustard leaves are available in Chinese and South-east Asian stores.

Per Portion Energy 58kcal/242kJ; Protein 5.6g; Carbohydrate 5.4g, of which sugars 5.2g; Fat 1.7g, of which saturates 0.3g; Cholesterol 0mg; Calcium 306mg; Fibre 4.5g; Sodium 252mg.

Fish and shellfish

Fish and shellfish

The Indonesians and the Filipinos are both sea-faring people with a penchant for everything nautical. In fact almost a tenth of the world's sailors come from the Philippines. With their crystal-clear waters and extensive coastlines, all the islands have a treasure trove of delectable seafood on tap, so it is hardly surprising to learn that fish and shellfish are an integral part of the cuisine of both archipelagos.

There is no end to the quantity and variety of fish available in the warm waters around Indonesia and the Philippines, where fishing is the primary industry, providing a livelihood for many people. Snapper, grouper, tuna, sardines, mackerel, perch, shark, anchovies, mussels, clams, oysters, lobsters, shrimp and crab are all fished from the deep Indian Ocean and in the shallower, warmer waters of the South China Sea, while carp, tilapia, and numerous catfish are found in the inland lakes and rivers, as well as in the flooded paddies.

Almost as astounding as the variety of fish is the sheer number and diversity of the fishing boats working the coastal waters, ranging from the small Polynesian-style dugout boats carved by small island communities to the large transport vessels. The traditional wooden sailing boats, used for transport and fishing, are still made by the Bugis in Sulawesi with timber from the jungles of Sumatra and East Kalimantan.

The basic diet of most Indonesians and Filipinos consists of plain boiled or steamed rice with fried fish and chillies to chew on. American soldiers stationed in the Philippines used to refer to the ubiquitous fried fish as "Filipino steak" as it cropped up so often. Fried for breakfast, fried for lunch, stewed for supper, simmered in broth, and fermented for the national fish sauce *patis*, fish is incorporated in some way into every meal of the day in the Philippines.

In Indonesia, deep-fried catfish is popular, particularly at food stalls where it is served with a spicy sauce made from chillies, peanuts and tomatoes in a dish called *pecel lele*. Grilled (broiled) fish and *pepes ikan* (fish cooked in banana leaves) are also popular street fish dishes. As fish is lighter on the stomach than meat, it is always served with rice, corn, or some other staple, such as sago, depending on where you are in the Philippines and Indonesia.

Above, from left to right *Fish cooked in banana leaves* (pepes ikan)*; lapu-lapu; sardines cooked in spicy coconut milk* (rempah-rempah).

In spite of the abundance, much of the prawns (shrimp) and squid that is caught in Indonesian waters goes to international markets as is too expensive for locals to afford. However, the tiny shrimp that are not exported are very cheap and are sold in vast quantities in the local markets, destined for a delicious dish of *nasi goreng* (Indonesian fried rice) or stir-fried water spinach (*kangkung*). They are also fermented and dried to make the pungent shrimp paste, *terasi*, which is added to many spice pastes and *sambals*. In South Sumatra and Kalimantan, the locals enjoy a regular supply of large, juicy river prawns which are often chargrilled with spices.

Whenever possible, Indonesians and Filipinos enjoy lobster and crab, including the meaty blue crab found off Palawan, the island famed for the giraffe and zebra brought in by Marcos for his private zoo. However, due to the expense, lobster and crab are often reserved for special occasions when they are steamed with oyster sauce, or deep-fried and served with a chilli *sambal* in Indonesia and spiked coconut vinegar in the Philippines.

When visiting Bali it is worth stopping off at the fishing district of Jamburan near Kuta, where the shore-front fish restaurants serve barracuda, lobster, snapper and prawns straight from the fishing buckets. Once you have chosen your fish, it is scaled and gutted, smeared with garlic and lime juice, and grilled (broiled) over smouldering coconut shells before your eyes. Just before serving, the fish is tossed in a chilli spice paste before being handed over for you to enjoy while you watch the water and the lights of fishing boats on the horizon.

In both the Philippines and Indonesia, many types of fish are sun-dried whole, or in chunks, fillets or strips in the open air. Generally, they are reconstituted before use by soaking them in water until soft. They are then deep-fried and served with rice. A typical Filipino breakfast will consist of fried garlic-flavoured rice served with fried dried fish.

In both cultures, dried fish is shredded or flaked to be used as a garnish, or added to soups, stews and stir-fries for their strong flavour. The type of dried fish available in the markets depends on the type of fish found in the local waters, although you can usually find sardines and anchovies. In the waters off Cebu in the Philippines, tiny *danggit* is much sought after for drying. More expensive than other dried fish, it is deep-fried straight from its packaging so that it is deliciously crisp and ready to be dipped into coconut vinegar. Butterflied and gutted before being dried in the sun, tiny dried *danggit* are also served deep-fried for breakfast with rice and eggs, served sunny side up – a speciality of Cebu.

Dried squid – which is often added to dishes during cooking without first being reconstituted in order to lend a unique, sweet and smoky flavour to soups and stocks – is also popular in the Philippines. Pleasantly chewy and slightly sweet to taste in its dried state, it is not uncommon to see people standing around the market stalls chewing on a piece of dried squid. It can also be used to make *toyong pusit satay* (found in the street snacks and satay section of this book), a delicious satay that is eaten at the beach and served with soft drinks or beer.

Above, from left to right *Stuffed squid* (relyenong pusit)*; lobster; yellow prawn curry* (udang huning)*.

Catfish with a spicy coconut sauce
Ikan asam pedes

Throughout South-east Asia, catfish is one of the most commonly cooked freshwater fish. In this popular Indonesian dish, the fish is simply fried and served with a fragrant and spicy sauce. Many Indonesian cooks make up jars of the basic spice paste, *base gede*, which they keep for flavouring simple meat, poultry and fish dishes like this one, instead of making a fresh spice paste every time. Serve the catfish with rice and pickled vegetables or a salad, with green mango or papaya.

1 First make the spice paste. Using a mortar and pestle, pound the shallots, garlic, chillies, galangal, turmeric and lemon grass to a coarse paste.

2 Heat the oil in a wok or heavy pan, stir in the paste and fry until it becomes fragrant and begins to colour. Add the *terasi*, tamarind paste and sugar and continue to stir until the paste darkens.

3 Stir the coconut milk and coconut cream into the spice paste and boil the mixture for about 10 minutes, until the coconut milk and cream separate, leaving behind an oily fragrant paste. Season the sauce with salt and pepper to taste.

Serves four

200ml/7fl oz/scant 1 cup coconut milk

30–45ml/2–3 tbsp coconut cream

30–45ml/2–3 tbsp rice flour, tapioca flour or cornflour (cornstarch)

5–10ml/1–2 tsp ground coriander

8 fresh catfish fillets

30–45ml/2–3 tbsp coconut, palm groundnut (peanut) or corn oil

salt and ground black pepper

1 lime, quartered, to serve

For the spice paste

2 shallots, chopped

2 garlic cloves, chopped

2–3 red chillies, seeded and chopped

25g/1oz galangal, chopped

15g/½ oz fresh turmeric, chopped, or 2.5ml/½ tsp ground turmeric

2–3 lemon grass stalks, chopped

15–30ml/1–2 tbsp palm or groundnut (peanut) oil

5ml/1 tsp *terasi* (Indonesian shrimp paste)

15ml/1 tbsp tamarind paste

5ml/1 tsp palm sugar

4 Meanwhile, on a large plate, mix the flour with the coriander and season with salt and pepper. Toss the catfish fillets in the flour so that they are lightly coated.

5 Heat the oil in a heavy frying pan and quickly fry the fillets for about 2 minutes on each side, until golden brown.

6 Transfer the catfish fillets to a warmed serving dish and served with the spicy coconut sauce and wedges of lime to squeeze over the fish.

Per Portion Energy 338kcal/1412kJ; Protein 38.1g; Carbohydrate 11.9g, of which sugars 4.9g; Fat 15.3g, of which saturates 5.7g; Cholesterol 92mg; Calcium 56mg; Fibre 0.9g; Sodium 190mg.

Sardines cooked in spicy coconut milk with herbs

Rempah-rempah

A fish dish based on coconut milk, *rempah-rempah* varies from region to region. In northern Sumatra, where the tolerance for chillies and spice is high, this dish is particularly fiery but is tempered by the inclusion of locally grown herbs. As a substitute for the local herbs, which are not available in the West, I have included fresh mint, basil and flat leaf parsley to cut the spice.

1 Using a mortar and pestle, pound the chillies, shallots, garlic, lemon grass and galangal to a paste.

2 Heat the oil in a wok or wide, heavy pan, stir in the coriander, cumin and fennel seeds and fry until they give off a nutty aroma. Add the paste and stir until it becomes fragrant and golden in colour. Add the chopped mint and parsley and stir for 1 minute then add the sugar and tamarind paste.

3 Carefully toss the fish into the pan, coating it in the paste, and pour in the coconut milk. Bring to the boil, then reduce the heat and cook gently for 10–15 minutes, until the fish is tender. Season the sauce with salt and pepper to taste.

4 Cover the bottom of a warmed serving dish with parsley and place the fish on top, then spoon the sauce over the top. Serve with a bowl of steamed rice or sago and stalks of fresh parsley and basil leaves to cut the spice.

Variation Whole mackerel or anchovies can be cooked in this way too. For a light, tasty meal, serve the fish with a green salad.

Serves four

6–8 red chillies, according to taste, seeded and chopped

4 shallots, chopped

4 garlic cloves, chopped

1 lemon grass stalk, chopped

25g/1oz galangal, chopped

30ml/2 tbsp coconut or palm oil

10ml/2 tsp coriander seeds

5ml/1 tsp cumin seeds

5ml/1 tsp fennel seeds

1 small bunch fresh mint leaves, finely chopped

1 small bunch fresh flat leaf parsley, finely chopped

15ml/1 tbsp palm sugar

15ml/1 tbsp tamarind paste

4 sardines or small mackerel, gutted, kept whole

300ml/½ pint/1¼ cups coconut milk

salt and ground black pepper

To serve

steamed rice or sago

1 large bunch fresh flat leaf parsley

fresh basil leaves

Per Portion Energy 287kcal/1199kJ; Protein 22.8g; Carbohydrate 11g, of which sugars 10.2g; Fat 17.2g, of which saturates 3.7g; Cholesterol 0mg; Calcium 167mg; Fibre 2.1g; Sodium 213mg.

Sumatran sour fish and star fruit stew
Pange ikan padang

Somewhere between a stew and a soup, this refreshing dish is just one of many variations on the theme of sour fish stew found throughout South-east Asia. The star fruit are added towards the end of cooking so that the fruit retains a bite.

1 Using a mortar and pestle, pound all the spice paste ingredients together to form a coarse paste. Heat the oil in a wok or wide, heavy pan, stir in the spice paste and fry until fragrant. Pour in the water and add the lemon grass and ginger. Bring to the boil, stirring all the time, then reduce the heat and simmer for 10 minutes.

2 Slip the fish steaks into the pan, making sure there is enough cooking liquid to cover the fish and adding more water if necessary. Simmer gently for 3–4 minutes, then add the star fruit and lime juice. Simmer for a further 2–3 minutes, until the fish is cooked.

3 Divide the fish and star fruit between four to six warmed serving bowls, spoon a little of the cooking liquid over the top, and garnish with basil leaves and a wedge of lime to squeeze over it. Serve with bowls of steamed rice, which is moistened by spoonfuls of the remaining cooking liquid.

Serves four to six

30ml/2 tbsp coconut or palm oil

about 900ml/1½ pints/3¾ cups water

2 lemon grass stalks, bruised

25g/1oz fresh root ginger, finely sliced

about 700g/1lb 9oz freshwater or saltwater fish, such as trout or sea bream, cut into thin steaks

2 firm star fruit (carambola), sliced

juice of 1–2 limes

For the spice paste

4 shallots, chopped

4 red chillies, seeded and chopped

2 garlic cloves, chopped

25g/1oz galangal, chopped

25g/1oz fresh turmeric, chopped

3–4 candlenuts, chopped

To serve

1 bunch fresh basil leaves

1 lime, cut into wedges

steamed rice

Per Portion Energy 240kcal/1001kJ; Protein 25.9g; Carbohydrate 7.3g, of which sugars 4.7g; Fat 12.1g, of which saturates 1.2g; Cholesterol 0mg; Calcium 27mg; Fibre 1.7g; Sodium 67mg.

Twice-cooked lapu-lapu
Escabeching lapu-lapu

It may seem like overkill but, in South-east Asia, it is not unusual to cook fish or meat twice to achieve the desired tender effect. In this Filipino dish from Cebu, the local fish, lapu-lapu, is first fried and then baked in a sauce. The fish itself is named after the local chief who fought Magellan during the battle of Mactan and it is, therefore, extremely popular on that island. Red snapper or sea bass are excellent substitutes.

1 Preheat the oven to 180°C/350°F/Gas 4. Rub the fish with salt. Heat 15ml/1 tbsp of the oil in a large frying pan, add the fish and fry on both sides for 2 minutes. Remove the fish from the pan and put aside.

2 Add the remaining oil to the pan, stir in the ginger, shallots, carrot and pepper and fry for 2–3 minutes until they begin to colour. Stir in the vinegar, soy sauce and sugar and season well with black pepper.

3 Put the fish in an ovenproof dish, spoon over the sauce and bake in the oven for 25–30 minutes. Garnish with the spring onions and serve with the lime wedges to squeeze over the fish.

Serves three to four

1–2 fresh lapu-lapu, sea bass or red snapper, gutted and cleaned, total weight 1.2–1.3kg/2½–3lb

30ml/2 tbsp palm or groundnut (peanut) oil

25g/1oz fresh root ginger, chopped

4 shallots, finely chopped

1 large carrot, diced

1 red (bell) pepper, seeded and diced

30ml/2 tbsp coconut vinegar

30ml/2 tbsp light soy sauce

10ml/2 tsp sugar

salt and ground black pepper

4 spring onions (scallions), finely sliced, to garnish

1 lime, cut into wedges, to serve

Per Portion Energy 237kcal/1001kJ; Protein 38.6g; Carbohydrate 10g, of which sugars 9.1g; Fat 5.1g, of which saturates 1g; Cholesterol 69mg; Calcium 100mg; Fibre 1.7g; Sodium 720mg.

Indonesian chargrilled fish with *sambal badjak*

Ikan bakar sambal badjak

In the coastal regions of Indonesia, grilling fish over charcoal is a common sight in the tourist resorts, in the villages, on the beach and by the roadside.

1 In a small bowl, mix the coconut oil, soy sauce, garlic and lime juice together. Put the fish in a shallow dish and slash the flesh at intervals with a sharp knife. Spoon the marinade over the fish and rub it into the skin and slashes. Leave for about 1 hour.

2 Meanwhile, prepare the *sambal*. Put the tamarind paste in a bowl, pour over the boiling water and leave to soak for 30 minutes. Strain into a separate bowl, pressing the paste through a sieve (strainer). Discard the solids and put the tamarind juice aside.

3 Using a mortar and pestle, pound the shallots, garlic, chillies, galangal and lime leaves to a coarse paste. Add the *terasi* and sugar and beat together until combined.

4 Heat the oil in a small wok, stir in the paste and fry for 2–3 minutes. Stir in the tamarind juice and boil until it reduces to a thick paste. Turn into a serving bowl.

5 Prepare the barbecue. Place the fish on the grill (broiler) and cook for 5 minutes each side, depending on the size of fish, basting it with any leftover marinade. Transfer the fish to a serving plate and serve with the *sambal* and boiled rice.

Serves four

30ml/2 tbsp coconut oil

60ml/4 tbsp dark soy sauce

2 garlic cloves, crushed

juice of 1 lime

1 whole large sea fish, such as grouper, red snapper, sea bass, large piece of sword fish, or 4 whole smaller fish, such as sardines, gutted and cleaned

cooked rice, to serve

For the *sambal badjak*

50g/2oz tamarind paste

150ml/¼ pint/⅔ cup boiling water

4 shallots, chopped

4 garlic cloves, chopped

4–6 red chillies, seeded and chopped

25g/1oz galangal, chopped

2 kaffir lime leaves, crumbled

10ml/2 tsp *terasi* (Indonesian shrimp paste)

10ml/2 tsp palm sugar

30ml/2 tbsp coconut or palm oil

Per Portion Energy 359kcal/1507kJ; Protein 42.3g; Carbohydrate 11.8g, of which sugars 9.3g; Fat 16.4g, of which saturates 2.3g; Cholesterol 75mg; Calcium 117mg; Fibre 1.4g; Sodium 1263mg.

Serves four

500g/1¼lb fresh fish fillets, cut into chunks

juice of 2 limes

4–6 shallots, chopped

2 red chillies, seeded and chopped

25g/1oz fresh root ginger, chopped

15g/½oz fresh turmeric, chopped

2 lemon grass stalks, chopped

3–4 candlenuts, ground

10ml/2 tsp palm sugar

salt

1–2 banana leaves, cut into 4 big squares

To serve

cooked rice

chilli *sambal*

Fish cooked in banana leaves
Pepes ikan

Cooking fish in banana leaves is a delightful method that can be found throughout South-east Asia. The banana leaves impart their own flavour and the fish remains beautifully succulent and fragrant.

1 In a large bowl, toss the fish fillets in the lime juice then leave to marinate at room temperature for 10–15 minutes.

2 Meanwhile, using a mortar and pestle, pound the shallots, chillies, ginger, turmeric and lemon grass to a coarse paste. Add the ground candlenuts and sugar and season with salt. Turn the paste into the bowl with the fish and toss to coat the fish in it.

3 Place the banana leaves on a flat surface and divide the fish mixture equally among them. Tuck in the sides and fold over the ends to form a neat parcel. Secure with string.

4 Place the banana leaf parcels in a steamer and cook for 25–30 minutes until tender. Serve hot with rice and a *sambal*.

Cook's tip Banana leaves are available in South-east Asian, Chinese and African food shops but, if you cannot find them, you can use aluminium foil instead and bake the fish in the oven at 180°C/350°F/Gas 4 instead of steaming them.

Per Portion Energy 225kcal/943kJ; Protein 27.6g; Carbohydrate 14.1g, of which sugars 10.4g; Fat 6.9g, of which saturates 1.2g; Cholesterol 58mg; Calcium 51mg; Fibre 2.5g; Sodium 79mg.

Milk fish stuffed with minced pork and peas
Relyenong bangus

Although milk fish is widely used throughout South-east Asia, it is regarded as the national fish of the Philippines. In this particular dish, the fish is bashed gently to loosen the skin, so that the flesh and bones can be removed from the fish while keeping it intact. The flesh is then cooked with pork and stuffed back into the empty fish skin so that it resembles a fish once more.

Serves three to four

1–2 fresh milk fish, sea bass or mackerel, gutted and cleaned, total weight 1.2–1.3kg/2½–3lb

15–30ml/1–2 tbsp palm or groundnut (peanut) oil

2–3 shallots, finely chopped

2 garlic cloves, finely chopped

115g/4oz minced (ground) pork

30ml/2 tbsp light soy sauce

400g/14oz can petit pois (baby peas), drained and rinsed

15ml/1 tbsp groundnut (peanut) or vegetable oil, for frying

15g/½oz/1 tbsp butter

salt and ground black pepper

To serve

45–60ml/3–4 tbsp coconut vinegar

2 red chillies, seeded and finely chopped

Variation If you prefer a spicier filling, add finely chopped fresh root ginger and fresh chillies to the pan with the garlic and the shallots.

1 Preheat the oven to 180°C/350°F/Gas 4. Put the fish on a flat surface and gently bash the body (not the head) with a rolling pin to soften the flesh and then, using your fingers, gently massage the skin away from the flesh. Be careful not to tear the skin. Using a sharp knife, make an incision on the underside of the fish, just below the gills, and squeeze the flesh from the tail end through this hole, keeping the head and backbone intact. Remove all the small bones from the flesh.

2 Heat the 15–30ml/1–2 tbsp palm or groundnut oil in a heavy frying pan, stir in the shallots and garlic and fry until they turn golden brown. Add the minced pork and fry for 2–3 minutes, and then stir in the fish flesh until mixed well together. Stir in the soy sauce and peas, and season well with salt and pepper.

3 Hold the empty fish skin in one hand and carefully stuff the fish and pork mixture back into the fish with the other hand. Secure the opening with a cocktail stick.

4 Heat the 15ml/1 tbsp groundnut or vegetable oil and the butter in a heavy frying pan and fry the stuffed fish on both sides, until well browned.

5 Remove the fish from the pan, wrap it in a sheet of aluminium foil and place it on a baking tray. Bake in the oven for about 35 minutes to allow the flavours to combine.

6 In a bowl, mix the coconut vinegar and chillies together. Remove the fish from the oven and cut it into thick, diagonal slices. Serve with the spiked coconut vinegar.

Per Portion Energy 397kcal/1665kJ; Protein 53.3g; Carbohydrate 12.7g, of which sugars 3.4g; Fat 15.4g, of which saturates 4.6g; Cholesterol 102mg; Calcium 116mg; Fibre 4.9g; Sodium 413mg.

Squid stuffed with breadcrumbs and Serrano ham

Relyenong pusit

This traditional Filipino dish of baby squid, stuffed with a tasty mixture of breadcrumbs and Spanish ham and cooked in wine, once again reflects the nation's colonial past. Whole fish can be stuffed in the same manner, using breadcrumbs or minced pork, such as *relyenong bangus*. A dish for celebrations and festival feasts, these stuffed squid are delicious served with rice or noodles and a seaweed salad.

1 To prepare the squid, use your fingers to pull off the head and reach into the body sac to pull out all the innards and the flat, thin bone. Rinse the sac inside and out and peel off the skin. Cut off the tentacles above the eyes, chop finely and reserve. Pat the sacs dry before stuffing.

2 Heat the oil in a heavy pan, stir in the shallots and garlic and fry until fragrant and beginning to colour. Add the reserved squid tentacles and Serrano ham and fry for 2–3 minutes. Stir in the paprika and chopped parsley and toss in the breadcrumbs to absorb all the juices and flavours. If the mixture is a little dry, splash in 15–30ml/ 1–2 tbsp of the wine. Leave the stuffing to cool.

3 Stuff the squid sacs with the breadcrumb filling and enclose each sac by threading a cocktail stick through the ends to prevent the filling from spilling out.

4 In a wide pan, bring the wine and stock to the boil. Drop in the bay leaves, reduce the heat and put the stuffed squid in the liquid. Cover the pan and simmer gently for 5–10 minutes until tender.

5 Transfer the squid to a warmed serving dish. Spoon some of the cooking juices over the squid, garnish with the reserved parsley leaves and serve with cooked rice.

Cook's tip If you are lucky enough to get the squid ink from the fishmonger, reserve about 90ml/6 tbsp to add to the wine during cooking.

Serves four

16 fresh baby squid

15–30ml/1–2 tbsp palm or groundnut (peanut) oil

2–3 shallots, finely chopped

2–3 garlic cloves, finely chopped

115g/4oz Serrano ham, finely chopped

5–10ml/1–2 tsp paprika

1 small bunch flat leaf parsley, finely chopped, reserving a few leaves to garnish

6–8 slices white bread, crusts removed, made into breadcrumbs

300ml/½ pint/1¼ cups dry white wine

300ml/½ pint/1¼ cups chicken stock

2–3 bay leaves

salt and ground black pepper

cooked rice, to serve

Per Portion Energy 344kcal/1449kJ; Protein 28.9g; Carbohydrate 25.5g, of which sugars 4.2g; Fat 9.6g, of which saturates 1.5g; Cholesterol 298mg; Calcium 104mg; Fibre 1.8g; Sodium 701mg.

Indonesian yellow prawn curry
Udang kuning

Serves four

30ml/2 tbsp coconut or palm oil

2 shallots, finely chopped

2 garlic cloves, finely chopped

2 red chillies, seeded and finely chopped

25g/1oz fresh turmeric, finely chopped, or 10ml/2 tsp ground turmeric

25g/1oz fresh root ginger, finely chopped

2 lemon grass stalks, finely sliced

10ml/2 tsp coriander seeds

10ml/2 tsp *terasi* (Indonesian shrimp paste)

1 red (bell) pepper, seeded and finely sliced

4 kaffir lime leaves

about 500g/1¼ lb fresh prawns (shrimp), shelled and deveined

400g/14oz can coconut milk

salt and ground black pepper

1 bunch fresh coriander (cilantro) leaves, roughly chopped, to garnish

To serve

cooked rice

4 fried shallots or fresh chillies, seeded and sliced lengthways

Colour is an important part of Indonesian food and the word *udang*, meaning "yellow", is used to describe this prawn dish as well as the popular rice dish, *nasi kuning*. Big, juicy prawns are particularly favoured for this dish in Bali and Java, but you can easily substitute them with scallops, squid or mussels, or a combination of all three.

1 Heat the oil in a wok or heavy pan, stir in the shallots, garlic, chillies, turmeric, ginger, lemon grass and coriander seeds and fry until fragrant. Stir in the *terasi* and cook the mixture for 2–3 minutes. Add the red pepper and lime leaves and stir-fry for 1 minute.

2 Toss the prawns into the pan. Pour in the coconut milk and bring to the boil. Season the curry with salt and pepper to taste.

3 Spoon the prawns on to a warmed serving dish and scatter the coriander leaves over the top to garnish. Serve with rice and fried shallots or sliced chillies on the side.

Per Portion Energy 230kcal/965kJ; Protein 26.4g; Carbohydrate 16g, of which sugars 13.5g; Fat 7.2g, of which saturates 1g; Cholesterol 263mg; Calcium 226mg; Fibre 2.7g; Sodium 519mg.

Steamed shellfish with tamarind dipping sauce
Pinakoloan na hipon

Steamed, boiled or grilled and served with dipping sauces, this is one of the favourite ways of eating shellfish in Indonesia and the Philippines. Whether it's a snack or a main dish, the locals never seem to tire of it, cracking shells open, sharing and dipping and chatting about life.

1 Scrub the lobsters, crabs, mussels and scallops or clams thoroughly under cold running water, removing any barnacles and seaweed. Rinse the prawns. Cut the spring onions into 2.5cm/1in pieces and then into strips.

2 Fill the bottom of two large steam pots with at least 5cm/2in water, then divide the spring onions, vinegar, garlic, ginger and peppercorns between them. Cover and bring to the boil. Place the large shellfish in one steamer and the smaller shellfish in the other. (You may need to steam them in batches and top up the water if it gets low.) Cover the pots and steam the lobsters and crabs for 10 minutes and the smaller shellfish for 5 minutes, until they turn opaque and the mussel, scallops or clam shells open.

3 Transfer the cooked shellfish to a large warmed serving dish and serve with the tamarind and lime sauce, accompanied by rice and a green papaya salad.

Serves four to six

2 whole lobsters, each weighing about 450g/1lb

3–4 medium crabs

24 mussels

24 scallops or clams

24 tiger prawns (shrimp)

6 spring onions (scallions)

150ml/¼ pint/⅔ cup coconut or rice vinegar

6 garlic cloves, crushed whole

about 50g/2oz fresh root ginger, finely sliced

6–8 black peppercorns

To serve

tamarind and lime dipping sauce

cooked rice

green papaya salad

Per Portion Energy 312kcal/1315kJ; Protein 61g; Carbohydrate 3.4g, of which sugars 0.5g; Fat 6.1g, of which saturates 1g; Cholesterol 309mg; Calcium 193mg; Fibre 0.6g; Sodium 769mg.

Filipino cured herring
Kinilaw

Generally served as an appetizer or snack in the Philippines, *kinilaw* can be made with many types of fish, including octopus, halibut and salmon, although mackerel and herring are particularly suitable. As with sushi or any other raw fish dish, the fish must be absolutely fresh. Cured in coconut vinegar and kalamansi lime juice, and flavoured with ginger and chillies, *kinilaw* is a delicious and refreshing snack.

1 Put the coconut vinegar, lime juice, ginger and chillies in a bowl and mix together. Season the mixture with salt and pepper.

2 Put the herring fillets in a shallow dish, scatter the shallots and green mango over the top, and pour the vinegar mixture over fish. Cover with clear film (plastic wrap) and leave to marinate in the refrigerator for 1–2 hours or overnight, turning the fish several times. Serve with coriander leaves scattered over the top and lime wedges.

Serves four

150ml/¼ pint/⅔ cup coconut vinegar

juice of 2 kalamansi limes

40g/1½oz fresh root ginger, grated

2 red chillies, seeded and finely sliced

8–10 herring fillets, cut into bitesize pieces

2 shallots, finely sliced

1 green mango, cut into julienne strips

salt and ground black pepper

1 small bunch fresh coriander (cilantro)

1 lime, cut into wedges

Per Portion Energy 408kcal/1699kJ; Protein 36.4g; Carbohydrate 5.9g, of which sugars 5.7g; Fat 26.7g, of which saturates 6.6g; Cholesterol 100mg; Calcium 160mg; Fibre 1.9g; Sodium 260mg.

Serves four

1 small bitter melon, cut into thick bitesize slices

1 small aubergine (eggplant), thickly sliced

4 spring onions (scallions), cut into 2.5cm/1in lengths

2 fresh green chillies, seeded and sliced

25g/1oz fresh root ginger, grated

4–6 black peppercorns

1 whole fish, gutted and cleaned, or fish fillets, total weight 500g/1¼ lb

250ml/8fl oz/1 cup coconut, rice or white wine vinegar

200ml/7fl oz/scant 1 cup water

30ml/2 tbsp light soy sauce

salt and ground black pepper

To serve

cooked rice

soy sauce

fresh chillies, seeded and sliced lengthways

Soused fish with aubergine and bitter melon
Pinaksiw

With their love of vinegar, this is an everyday dish for many Filipinos. Served with rice it is normally eaten for lunch or for the morning and afternoon *merienda*. The local milkfish is often cooked this way but trout, mackerel, herring or sea bass are just as suitable.

1 Arrange the bitter melon and aubergine in the bottom of a wide, heavy pan. Sprinkle the spring onions, chillies, ginger and peppercorns over the top. Place the whole fish, or arrange the fillets, over the vegetables.

2 In a bowl, mix the vinegar, water and soy sauce together then pour the mixture over the fish and vegetables. Season the dish with a little salt and lots of black pepper Bring to the boil, reduce the heat, cover and simmer gently for about 1 hour.

3 Transfer the fish to a serving dish and spoon the vegetables and cooking liquid over and around the fish. Leave to cool. Serve the fish with rice, soy sauce and chillies.

Per Portion Energy 151kcal/636kJ; Protein 20.7g; Carbohydrate 8.5g, of which sugars 8.3g; Fat 4g, of which saturates 0.9g; Cholesterol 80mg; Calcium 54mg; Fibre 1.2g; Sodium 647mg.

Meat and poultry

Meat and poultry

The culinary cultures of Indonesia and the Philippines are fabulous for people who enjoy eating meat, although the use of pork differs markedly between the two countries. While the largely Christian Filipinos cannot wait to cook a delectable pork *adobo* (chicken and pork cooked in vinegar and ginger) or spit-roast a whole pig, most Indonesians are Muslims and, therefore, forbidden from eating pork.

The exception to this absence of pork from the menu in Indonesia occurs in Bali, where Hindus enjoy a spit-roast pig; the Batak of Sumatra; the Toraja of Sulawesi and the Chinese communities throughout the region. For a Filipino, however, life would be unbearable without pork, which is the chosen meat of fiestas and all forms of celebration. Cooked in stews and combined with noodles and rice, every part of the pig is used, and the traditional by-products include the *longaniza* (spicy cured sausage) and *bagnet* (crispy fried pork belly).

The few non-pork eaters in the Philippines include the Muslims of Mindanao and the Moros of the Luzon, both of whom eat the flesh of goats, buffalo, chickens and ducks, but not pork. Among the exotic meats available in Indonesia you will find dog, bear and lizard, particularly in north Sulawesi and Sumatra. Believed to be warming for the blood, dog is added to many stews, so watch out!

In both island archipelagos, cows and buffalo are valued for their meat, milk and hide, as well as in their roles as beasts of burden. In Indonesia, cows are found on the drier islands of Madura and Nusa Tenggara, whereas buffalo tend to thrive in areas of high rainfall. In spite of the predominant Hindu culture in Bali, many of the Balinese eat beef, apart from the Hindu priests and some devout followers who adhere to the belief that the cow is sacred.

One of the best known Indonesian recipes is *rendang* (slow-cooked buffalo in coconut milk), a deliciously tender curry. In Yogyakarta, buffalo is used to make *krecek* (buffalo skin crackling), which is served as an accompaniment to the local *gudeg* (jackfruit curry). In the Philippines, beef and buffalo meat are often cooked in stews and curries, but the prized cut is the oxtail. Filipinos adore their beloved dish of *kare kare* (oxtail braised in peanut sauce).

Above, from left to right *Stuffed beef roll* (morcon)*; green olives; buffalo in coconut milk* (rendang).

Mutton and goat are cooked in a number of stews and curries, such as the spicy, coconut milk curry (*gulai kambing*) in Indonesia and *kaldareta* (Spanish-style lamb stew with green olives) in the Philippines. Mutton or lamb is also marinated in spices to make *sate kambing* (lamb satay) and a whole goat or lamb is often spit-roasted, or baked in an earthen pit, for communal feasts. As the Indonesians enjoy strong tastes and odours, they often prefer goat meat to mutton or lamb. Other meats include rabbits, which are sold live in the markets, and usually destined for a spicy *sate kilinci* (rabbit satay) in Indonesia or paella in the Philippines.

When it comes to butchering the meat, traditional Islamic restrictions apply to the stricter Muslim populations of both cultures. In order to render the meat *halal*, the animal must first be slaughtered by cutting the throat and draining the blood, then all traces of blood must be removed from the meat by soaking it in water. In direct contrast, the neighbouring Catholic Filipinos and the tribal Dayaks of Kalimantan revel in stews where the meat is cooked in its own blood, such as the Filipino dish *dinuguan baboy* (pork and liver cooked in blood).

Every conceivable part of the pig is used in Filipino cooking and the innards of buffalo, cows and sheep also find their way into local soups and stews. In Sumatra, *tembusu*, a sausage made from buffalo intestines stuffed with egg and herbs, is a speciality, and liver is regarded throughout Indonesia as the "cradle of one's emotions". The Indonesian expression for "take care" is *hati-hati*, which literally translates as "liver-liver".

In general, the meat of these islands is not very well hung, so most cuts require tenderizing before cooking. In Indonesia, this is done by marinating the meat in a spice paste or by slow-cooking, whereas the Filipinos rely on coconut vinegar or kalamansi limes as marinades, or they boil the meat prior to cooking. Another local method is to use dried papaya seeds, which are crushed and rubbed all over the meat to soften it.

Chickens and ducks are a feature of every village. In the Hindu communities of Bali, roosters are carried around in baskets and groomed for cockfights, which are a feature of Balinese temple festivals. Ducks receive special treatment too, as are often shepherded to the rice paddies to swim and to feast on the meaty insects. In Indonesia, typical chicken dishes include *ayam goreng* (filipino street chicken), *opor ayam* (chicken in a coconut curry with pepper), and *sate ayam*, the popular chicken satay found at street stalls. Little is wasted on a chicken as the Javanese specialize in a tasty chicken liver satay and the Kalimantan version of the popular soup, *bakso*, includes chicken claws.

In Bali, the duck speciality is *bebek betutu* (Balinese smoked duck), which is prepared by stuffing the duck with spices, wrapping it in banana leaves and cooking it in a pit over smouldering coconut husks. The word for duck differs in Sumatra, where they refer to it as *itik* and make a delicious duck coconut curry, *gulai itik*. The Filipinos have their own tasty fried chicken, which is marinated in beer and garlic before frying. This is a great favourite at street stalls and family get-togethers.

Above, from left to right *Goat curry* (kambing kare)*; spice paste; Indonesian fried chicken* (ayam goreng)*.*

Spanish-style lamb stew with green olives
Kaldareta

Pork is the principal meat in the Philippines, closely followed by chicken and then beef, but lamb and goat are not widely eaten. However, in the northern Luzon the mountain tribes eat lamb and goat in hearty stews. Drawing from Spanish tradition, the meat is first marinated in a local alcohol, such as the sweet, port-like *basi*, made, from fermented sugar cane juice, to tenderize the meat and tame the strong taste of goat, and then browned before braising. The green olives that are native to the area are used in this dish.

1 First make the marinade by mixing all the ingredients together in a large bowl. Add the lamb, toss in the marinade, then cover the bowl with clear film (plastic wrap) and leave to marinate in the refrigerator for at least 6 hours or overnight.

2 Using a slotted spoon to strain the marinade, lift the lamb out of the marinade and put it in another large bowl. Put the marinade aside.

3 Heat the oil and butter in a wok with a lid or a large flameproof casserole. Add the meat, in batches if necessary, and fry until browned on all sides. Using a slotted spoon, lift the browned meat out of the pan and put aside.

4 Add the onions, garlic, chillies and peppers to the remaining oil in the pan and fry for about 5 minutes until they begin to colour. Stir in the paprika and sugar and return the meat to the pan. Add the tomatoes, tomato paste, bay leaves and olives. Pour in the reserved marinade and the water and bring to the boil. Reduce the heat, cover the pan and simmer gently for about 2 hours, adding a little extra water if the cooking liquid reduces too much.

5 Season the stew with salt and pepper to taste. Sprinkle with chopped parsley to garnish and serve with rice.

Serves four

900g/2lb boneless leg or shoulder of lamb, cut into bitesize cubes

45ml/3 tbsp groundnut (peanut) oil

15g/½oz/1 tbsp butter

2 red onions, thickly sliced

8 garlic cloves, crushed whole

2–3 red or green chillies, seeded and sliced

2 red or green (bell) peppers, seeded and sliced

5–10ml/1–2 tsp paprika

15–30ml/1–2 tbsp palm or cane sugar

400g/14oz can plum tomatoes, drained

15–30ml/1–2 tbsp tomato purée (paste)

2–3 bay leaves

225g/8oz small green olives, with stones (pits)

300ml/½ pint/1¼ cups water

salt and ground black pepper

1 bunch fresh flat leaf parsley, roughly chopped, to garnish

cooked rice, to serve

For the marinade

250ml/8fl oz/1 cup red wine

250ml/8fl oz/1 cup port

120ml/4fl oz/½ cup coconut or rice vinegar

1 onion, roughly sliced

2 garlic cloves, crushed whole

8 black peppercorns

2–3 bay leaves

Cook's tip Choose olives with stones (pits) in them as then they remain intact when cooked and add to the flavour of the stew.

Per Portion Energy 654kcal/2722kJ; Protein 47.4g; Carbohydrate 19.2g, of which sugars 16.7g; Fat 43.6g, of which saturates 15.8g; Cholesterol 179mg; Calcium 93mg; Fibre 5.4g; Sodium 1498mg.

Slow-cooked buffalo in coconut milk
Rendang

Serves six

1kg/2¼lb buffalo or beef, such as topside (pot roast) or rump (round) steak, cut into bitesize cubes

15ml/1 tbsp tamarind paste

90ml/6 tbsp water

115g/4oz fresh coconut, grated, or desiccated (dry unsweetened shredded) coconut

45ml/3 tbsp coconut, corn or groundnut (peanut) oil

2 onions, sliced

3 lemon grass stalks, halved and bruised

2 cinnamon sticks

3–4 lime leaves

1.2 litres/2 pints/5 cups coconut milk

15ml/1 tbsp sugar

salt and ground black pepper

For the spice paste

8–10 dried red chillies

8 shallots, chopped

4–6 garlic cloves, chopped

50g/2oz galangal, chopped

25g/1oz fresh turmeric, chopped

15ml/1 tbsp coriander seeds

10ml/2 tsp cumin seeds

5ml/1 tsp black peppercorns

To serve

15ml/1 tbsp corn or groundnut (peanut) oil

6–8 shallots, sliced

cooked rice and a salad

Variation This is a good recipe to use for venison and other game, as the slow-cooking renders the meat tender, succulent and very tasty.

This is one of Indonesia's most popular and best known meat dishes. Traditionally made with the meat of water buffalo, although a good cut of well-hung, prime beef is equally delicious, the dish is cooked slowly to achieve the required tenderness and create a rich, thick sauce.

1 First make the spice paste. Soak the dried chillies in warm water for 30 minutes, until soft. Drain, remove the seeds then squeeze the chillies until dry. Using a mortar and pestle or a food processor, grind the soaked chillies, shallots, garlic, galangal and turmeric to a smooth paste. Turn the mixture into a small bowl.

2 In a small, heavy frying pan, dry-fry the coriander, cumin seeds and peppercorns, until they give off a nutty aroma. Using a mortar and pestle, or an electric spice grinder, grind the dry-fried spices to a powder then stir into the spice paste.

3 Put the buffalo or beef in a large bowl, add the spice paste and mix together until coated. Leave to marinate, at room temperature or in the refrigerator, for at least 2 hours if using buffalo or 1 hour if using beef.

4 Meanwhile, put the tamarind paste and water in a bowl and leave to soak for about 30 minutes until soft. Using a heavy frying pan, dry-fry the grated coconut until it is brown and gives off a nutty aroma. Using a mortar and pestle, or a food processor, grind the dry-fried coconut until it resembles brown sugar. Put aside. Squeeze the tamarind to help soften it and then strain to extract the juice. Discard the pulp.

5 Heat the oil in a wok with a lid or large, flameproof casserole. Add the onions, lemon grass, cinnamon stick and lime leaves, and fry for 5–10 minutes until the onions begin to colour.

6 Add the beef with all the spice paste and fry, stirring all the time, until lightly browned. Pour in the coconut milk and tamarind juice and bring to the boil, stirring all the time. Reduce the heat and simmer gently for 2–4 hours for beef (4 hours for buffalo) until the sauce begins to thicken.

7 Stir in the sugar and the ground coconut, cover and continue to simmer very gently, for 4 hours if using buffalo meat and between 2–4 hours if using beef, stirring occasionally, until the meat is tender and the reduced sauce is very thick.

8 Meanwhile, heat the oil in a heavy frying pan, stir in the shallots and fry for about 10 minutes until almost caramelized. Drain on kitchen paper and put aside.

9 When the meat is tender, season to taste and spoon it onto a warmed serving dish. Sprinkle the fried shallots over the top and serve immediately with rice and a salad.

Per Portion Energy 494kcal/2064kJ; Protein 40.6g; Carbohydrate 20.9g, of which sugars 18.8g; Fat 28.2g, of which saturates 17g; Cholesterol 97mg; Calcium 95mg; Fibre 3.9g; Sodium 335mg.

Oxtail braised in peanut sauce
Kare kare

In true Spanish style, many of the Filipino stews are rich and hearty. The Filipinos love oxtail and cook it in more ways than any other country in South-east Asia. The peanuts enrich the sauce and give this dish its own character.

1 Heat a heavy, flameproof casserole, add the oxtail pieces and cook until browned on both sides. You may need to add a little oil but generally the oxtail renders sufficient fat. Transfer the meat to a plate.

2 Heat the fat from the oxtail, adding a little oil if there is not enough, stir in the onion and garlic and fry until they begin to brown. Add the tomatoes, *patis* and bay leaves and pour in the stock.

3 Return the oxtail to the pan. Bring to the boil, reduce the heat, cover and simmer gently for 4–5 hours, until tender, adding a little extra water if necessary.

4 Skim the fat off the top and, using a slotted spoon, lift the oxtail on to a plate. Stir the rice flour and ground peanuts into the stew and whisk until fairly smooth. Add the banana heart, snake beans and aubergine and simmer for 5–6 minutes, until tender.

5 Season the stew with salt and pepper to taste. Return the oxtail to the pan and simmer for a further 5 minutes. Serve hot, with rice, a bowl of *bagoong* to spoon over the stew and slices of green mango.

Serves four

1.5kg/1lb 5oz oxtail, cut into 2.5cm/1in pieces

corn or groundnut (peanut) oil (if necessary)

1 onion, sliced

4–5 garlic cloves, crushed whole

400g/14oz can plum tomatoes

30ml/2 tbsp *patis* (fish sauce)

2–3 bay leaves

1.5 litres/2½ pints/6¼ cups beef stock

40g/1½oz rice flour, dry-roasted

115g/4oz roasted unsalted peanuts, finely ground

1 banana heart (blossom), sliced into bitesize pieces

12 snake beans (yardlong beans), cut into 2.5cm/1in pieces

1 aubergine (eggplant), cut into bitesize pieces

salt and ground black pepper

To serve

cooked rice

60–90ml/4–6 tbsp *bagoong* (shrimp sauce)

1 firm green mango, finely sliced

Variations This dish can also be made with meaty beef ribs or shin (shank) of veal. Powdered peanuts, available from South-east Asian supermarkets, can be used instead of the ground peanuts.

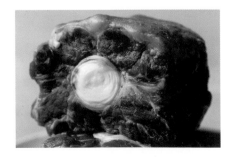

Per Portion Energy 885kcal/3693kJ; Protein 85.5g; Carbohydrate 19.2g, of which sugars 8.4g; Fat 52g, of which saturates 18.5g; Cholesterol 281mg; Calcium 89mg; Fibre 5.3g; Sodium 958mg.

Serves four to six

30–45ml/2–3 tbsp groundnut (peanut) or corn oil

1 onion, chopped

2 garlic cloves, chopped

40g/1½oz fresh root ginger, chopped

2 x 175g/6oz chorizo sausages, cut diagonally into bitesize pieces

700g/1lb 9oz lean rump (round) beef, cut into bitesize pieces

4 tomatoes, skinned, seeded and quartered

900ml/1½ pints/3¾ cups beef or chicken stock

2 plantains, sliced diagonally

2 x 400g/14oz cans chickpeas, rinsed and drained

salt and ground black pepper

1 small bunch fresh coriander (cilantro) leaves, roughly chopped, to garnish

To serve

corn oil, for deep-frying

1–2 firm bananas or 1 plantain, sliced diagonally

stir-fried greens

Beef and chorizo stew with plantain and chickpeas
Pochero

This dish can be made with beef, chicken or pork, all of which are cooked the same way. In the Philippines, this dish is generally made with the small, firm *saba* bananas, which can be substituted with plantains.

1 Heat the oil in a wok with a lid or a flameproof casserole, stir in the onion, garlic and ginger and fry until they begin to brown. Add the chorizo sausages and beef and fry until they begin to brown. Add the tomatoes and pour in the stock. Bring to the boil, reduce the heat, cover and simmer gently for about 45 minutes.

2 Add the plantains and chickpeas to the stew and cook for a further 20–25 minutes, adding a little extra water if the cooking liquid reduces too much.

3 Meanwhile, heat enough oil for deep-frying in a wok or large, shallow pan. Deep-fry the bananas or plantain, in batches, for about 3 minutes, until crisp and golden brown. Remove from the pan using a slotted spoon, drain on kitchen paper then arrange in a serving dish or basket.

4 Season the stew with salt and pepper to taste and sprinkle with chopped coriander leaves to garnish. Serve with the deep-fried bananas or plantain and stir-fried greens.

Per Portion Energy 583kcal/2441kJ; Protein 40.5g; Carbohydrate 35.8g, of which sugars 6.2g; Fat 31.9g, of which saturates 11.1g; Cholesterol 91mg; Calcium 104mg; Fibre 6.1g; Sodium 778mg.

Stuffed beef roll
Morcon

In this unusual recipe, beef is filled with chorizo, gherkins and hard-boiled eggs before being rolled, cooked and cut into slices.

1 Using a sharp knife, cut the steak lengthways through the centre but not all the way to the base, so that it opens out into a wide, flat steak. Rub the garlic and lemon juice all over the steak and season with salt and pepper.

2 Arrange the sliced egg, chorizo, gherkins and ham in rows down the steak, leaving a 1cm/½in border around the edge. Carefully roll up the steak and secure with a piece of string to make sure that the filling doesn't escape during cooking.

3 Heat the oil in a heavy pan, add the meat and fry until browned on all sides. Remove the meat from the pan and drain on kitchen paper. Add the vinegar, soy sauce, tomatoes, sugar, water and bay leaves to the pan and bring to the boil. Lower the heat. Return the meat to the pan. Cover and simmer for about 1 hour, until the meat is tender. Add more water to the pan if it becomes too dry during cooking.

4 Lift the meat out of the pan and place on a carving dish or board. Boil the liquid in the pan for 3–4 minutes, to thicken slightly, and season with pepper. Meanwhile, remove the string from the meat and carve into thick slices. Arrange the slices on a serving dish. Serve with the sauce drizzled over them or served separately in a bowl.

Serves four to six

1kg/2¼lb thin skirt (flank) steak, in one piece

2–3 garlic cloves, crushed

juice of 1½ lemon

2 hard-boiled eggs, finely sliced

1–2 chorizo sausages, each weighing about 175g/6oz, finely sliced diagonally

1–2 large sweet gherkins, finely sliced diagonally

2 slices cooked honey-roast ham, cut into strips

30ml/2 tbsp groundnut (peanut) or palm oil

30ml/2 tbsp coconut or white wine vinegar

30–45ml/2–3 tbsp soy sauce

400g can chopped tomatoes

15ml/1 tbsp palm sugar

about 300ml/½ pint/1¼ cups water

2 bay leaves

salt and ground black pepper

Per Portion Energy 558kcal/2323kJ; Protein 47.8g; Carbohydrate 12.3g, of which sugars 6.4g; Fat 35.6g, of which saturates 13.3g; Cholesterol 188mg; Calcium 56mg; Fibre 1.1g; Sodium 1065mg.

Serves four to six

1 leafy green cabbage

15–30ml/1–2 tbsp palm or groundnut (peanut) oil

10ml/2 tsp coriander seeds

2 shallots, finely chopped

2 garlic cloves, finely chopped

2–3 red chillies, seeded and finely chopped

25g/1oz galangal, finely chopped

2–3 spring onions (scallions), finely chopped

10ml/2 tsp palm sugar

2–3 tomatoes, skinned, seeded and finely chopped

30ml/2 tbsp coconut cream

1 small bunch fresh coriander (cilantro) leaves, finely chopped

225g/8oz minced (ground) pork

50g/2oz pig's liver, finely chopped

50g/2oz pig's heart, finely chopped

salt and ground black pepper

kecap manis (Indonesian sweet soy sauce), for dipping

Cabbage leaves stuffed with sweet and spicy pork
Piong duku babi

In South-east Asia, spicy pork or shellfish mixtures are often wrapped in leaves and steamed, or stuffed into bamboo stems and smoked over open fires.

1 First prepare the cabbage leaves. Carefully pull the cabbage apart so that you have about 20 whole leaves. Steam or blanch the leaves to soften, drain and refresh under cold running water. Cut off any thick stems, stack the leaves and put aside.

2 Heat the oil in a wok or heavy pan, stir in the coriander seeds and fry for 1 minute. Add the shallots, garlic, chillies, galangal, spring onions and sugar and stir-fry until they begin to colour. Stir in the tomatoes, coconut cream and coriander leaves and cook for 5 minutes, allowing the liquid to bubble, until the mixture resembles a thick sauce or paste. Season the mixture with salt and pepper and turn into a bowl. Leave to cool.

3 Add the minced pork and liver and, using your hand or a fork, mix well together. Place a cabbage leaf on a flat surface in front of you and place a spoonful of the mixture in the centre. Fold in the sides of the leaf and roll it up into a log, making sure the meat is enclosed. Repeat with the remaining leaves.

4 Place the stuffed leaves in a steamer, seam–side down, and steam for 25–30 minutes, until the meat is cooked. Serve hot with *kecap manis* for dipping.

Per Portion Energy 183kcal/764kJ; Protein 12.6g; Carbohydrate 7.3g, of which sugars 7g; Fat 11.8g, of which saturates 5g; Cholesterol 56mg; Calcium 55mg; Fibre 2.2g; Sodium 53mg.

Serves four

30–60ml/2–4 tbsp palm, coconut or groundnut (peanut) oil

10ml/2 tsp *terasi* (Indonesian shrimp paste)

15ml/1 tbsp palm sugar

5ml/1 tsp coriander seeds

5ml/1 tsp cumin seeds

2.5ml/½ tsp grated nutmeg

2.5ml/½ tsp ground black pepper

2–3 lemon grass stalks, halved and bruised

700g/1lb 9oz boneless shoulder or leg of goat, or lamb, cut into bitesize pieces

400g/14oz can coconut milk

200ml/7fl oz/scant 1 cup water (if necessary)

12 snake beans (yardlong beans)

1 bunch fresh coriander (cilantro) leaves, roughly chopped

For the spice paste

2–3 shallots, chopped

2–3 garlic cloves, chopped

3–4 chillies, seeded and chopped

25g/1oz galangal, chopped

40g/1½oz fresh turmeric, chopped, or 10ml/2 tsp ground turmeric

1 lemon grass stalk, chopped

2–3 candlenuts, finely ground

To serve

cooked rice

2–3 chillies, seeded and finely chopped

Cook's tip Indonesians love strong culinary tastes and odours but, if you find the taste and smell of goat's meat a little overpowering, then blanch it in boiling water for 10 minutes and drain it before adding to the curry pan.

Javanese goat curry
Kambing kare

Throughout Indonesia, lean goat's meat is more commonly used than lamb or mutton, although lamb could be used as substitute in this recipe. Slow-cooked on the hob with lots of pungent spices, the tender, tasty goat's meat is customarily served with rice and a pickle or sambal. This recipe is from Java where the dish is also known as *gulai kambing*, but there are many local variations throughout the Indonesian archipelago.

1 First make the spice paste. Using a pestle and mortar or a food processor, grind the shallots, garlic, chillies, galangal, turmeric, lemon grass and candlenuts to a paste.

2 Heat 15–30ml/1–2 tbsp of the oil in a heavy pan, stir in the spice paste and fry until fragrant and beginning to colour. Add the *terasi* and palm sugar and continue to stir-fry for 1–2 minutes, until the paste has deepened in colour but is not too dark.

3 Heat the remaining 15–30ml/1–2 tbsp oil in a large, flameproof casserole. Stir in the coriander seeds, cumin seeds, nutmeg and black pepper, then add the spice paste and lemon grass. Stir-fry for 2–3 minutes, until the mixture is dark and fragrant.

4 Stir the meat into the pan, making sure that it is well coated in the paste. Pour in the coconut milk and water, bring to the boil, then reduce the heat, cover and simmer gently for about 3 hours, until the meat is very tender.

5 Add the snake beans and cook for a further 10–15 minutes. Check the meat from time to time and add the water if the curry becomes too dry.

6 Toss some of the coriander leaves into the curry and season with salt and pepper to taste. Turn the curry into a warmed serving dish and sprinkle the remaining coriander leaves over the top. Serve with rice and chopped chillies.

Per Portion Energy 450kcal/1877kJ; Protein 37.9g; Carbohydrate 10.8g, of which sugars 9.1g; Fat 28.7g, of which saturates 10.3g; Cholesterol 146mg; Calcium 129mg; Fibre 2.4g; Sodium 375mg.

Balinese smoked duck
Bebek betutu

In the villages of Indonesia, this dish of slow-cooked, tender duck is prepared for celebratory feasts. Smeared with spices and herbs and tightly wrapped in banana or pandanus leaves, the duck is smoked in the embers of a fire made from coconut husks until the aromatic meat is so tender it falls off the bone.

1 First make the spice paste. Using a mortar and pestle or a food processor, grind all the ingredients, except the *terasi* and water, together to form a smooth paste. Add the *terasi* and water and mix together until the mixture resembles a thick paste.

2 Preheat the oven to 160°C/325°F/Gas 3. Rub the spice paste all over the duck, inside and out, and sprinkle with salt and pepper. Place the duck in the centre of the banana leaf or a sheet of aluminium foil. If using a banana leaf, secure it with string. If using foil, tuck in the short sides and fold the long sides over the top to form a parcel. Place the parcel in a roasting tin.

3 Roast the duck for 4–5 hours, then open the parcel to reveal the top of the duck and roast for a further 30–45 minutes to brown the skin. Serve immediately.

Serves four

1.8kg/4lb oven-ready duck

1 large banana leaf or aluminium foil

salt and ground black pepper

For the spice paste

6–8 shallots, chopped

4 garlic cloves, chopped

4 chillies, seeded and chopped

25g/1oz fresh root ginger, chopped

50g/2oz fresh turmeric, chopped, or 25ml/1½ tbsp ground turmeric

2 lemon grass stalks, chopped

4 lime leaves, crumbled

4 candlenuts, chopped

10ml/2 tsp coriander seeds

15ml/1 tbsp *terasi* (Indonesian shrimp paste)

15–30ml/1–2 tbsp water

Cook's tip The duck can be wrapped in banana leaves or aluminium foil and baked in the oven.

Per Portion Energy 234kcal/982kJ; Protein 26.9g; Carbohydrate 12.8g, of which sugars 8.4g; Fat 8.8g, of which saturates 2.7g; Cholesterol 135mg; Calcium 75mg; Fibre 3g; Sodium 161mg.

Serves four

12 chicken thighs or drumsticks, or 12 legs, separated into thighs and drumsticks

30ml/2 tbsp *kecap manis* (Indonesian sweet soy sauce)

150ml/¼ pint/⅔ cup water

vegetable oil, for deep-frying

salt and ground black pepper

For the spice paste

2 shallots, chopped

4 garlic cloves, chopped

50g/2oz fresh root ginger, chopped

25g/1oz fresh turmeric, chopped

2 lemon grass stalks, chopped

Variation *Kecap manis* is soy sauce sweetened with palm sugar and is available in Chinese and Asian supermarkets. However, if you cannot find it, you can substitute it with the same quantity of dark soy sauce and 15ml/1 tbsp sugar.

Indonesian fried chicken
Ayam goreng

Indonesian fried chicken puts Western fried chicken to shame. First of all the chicken is cooked in spices and flavourings to ensure a depth of flavour and then it is simply deep-fried to form a crisp, golden skin. Serve with a *sambal* or pickle for a delicious snack or, for a tasty meal, accompany it with yellow or fragrant coconut rice and a salad.

1 First make the spice paste. Using a mortar and pestle or a food processor, grind the shallots, garlic, ginger, turmeric and lemon grass to a paste.

2 Put the chicken pieces in a large, flameproof casserole and smear the spice paste over them. Add the *kecap manis* and the water to the casserole, bring to the boil, then reduce the heat and simmer for about 25 minutes, turning the chicken occasionally, until all the liquid has evaporated. You need the chicken to be dry before deep–frying but the spices should be sticking to it. Season the chicken pieces with salt and pepper.

3 Heat enough oil for deep-frying in a wok. Add the chicken pieces, in batches, and fry for 6–8 minutes until golden brown and crisp. Remove from the wok with a slotted spoon, drain on kitchen paper and serve hot.

Per Portion Energy 410kcal/1719kJ; Protein 60.8g; Carbohydrate 4.6g, of which sugars 3.4g; Fat 16.6g, of which saturates 2.4g; Cholesterol 175mg; Calcium 26mg; Fibre 0.7g; Sodium 686mg.

Visayan roast chicken with lemon grass
Inasal na manok

Throughout the Visayan islands, the aroma of chicken grilling with lemon grass and ginger will make you feel positively famished. Spit-roasted in the streets or oven-roasted in the home kitchen for celebratory feasts, *inasal na manok* can be found all over the Philippines, but on the Visayan islands, where the lemon grass grows wild in abundance, it is particularly delicious. In this recipe from Cebu, the chicken is roasted in the oven.

1 Preheat the oven to 180°C/350°F/Gas 4. First make the paste. Using a mortar and pestle, grind the ginger, lemon grass and garlic to a coarse paste. Beat in the soy sauce and lime juice. Add the sugar and mix until it dissolves. Season with pepper.

2 Put the chicken on a flat surface and gently massage the skin to loosen it from the flesh. Make a few incisions in the skin and flesh and rub the ginger and lemon grass paste into the slits and under the skin.

3 Put the chicken in a roasting pan and stuff it with four of the lemon grass stalks. Arrange the sweet potatoes around the chicken in the roasting pan with the remaining lemon grass stalks and the ginger. Drizzle the oil over the chicken and potatoes and season with salt and pepper.

4 Roast the chicken and sweet potatoes in the oven for 1–1¼ hours, until the juices run clear. Check after 50 minutes to make sure the sugar in the paste is not burning and baste the potatoes in the roasting juices. The potatoes should caramelize well in their own natural sugar.

5 Meanwhile, make the sweet chilli vinegar. Put the vinegar and sugar in a small bowl and stir until the sugar dissolves. Stir in the chillies and put aside.

6 When the chicken and potatoes are cooked, serve immediately with the sweet chilli vinegar to splash over it and a green papaya salad.

Serves four to six

1 organic chicken, total weight about 1.25kg/2lb 12oz

6 lemon grass stalks, bruised

2–3 large sweet potatoes, peeled or unpeeled, cut into wedges

40g/1½oz fresh root ginger, cut into matchsticks

30–45ml/2–3 tbsp coconut or groundnut (peanut) oil

salt and ground black pepper

green papaya salad, to serve

For the paste

90g/3½oz fresh root ginger, chopped

2–3 lemon grass stalks, chopped

3 garlic cloves, chopped

90ml/6 tbsp light soy sauce

juice of 1 kalamansi lime or 1 ordinary lime or lemon

30ml/2 tbsp palm or muscavado sugar

ground black pepper

For the sweet chilli vinegar

90ml/6 tbsp coconut vinegar

15–30ml/1–2 tbsp granulated or soft brown sugar

1–2 red chillies, seeded and chopped

Per Portion Energy 434kcal/1812kJ; Protein 26.2g; Carbohydrate 28.6g, of which sugars 12.6g; Fat 24.6g, of which saturates 6.5g; Cholesterol 128mg; Calcium 42mg; Fibre 2.5g; Sodium 1209mg.

Indonesian chicken and prawn salad
Ayam pelalah

Spicy and refreshing chicken and/or shellfish salads are popular at Indonesian food stalls and as part of large, celebratory feasts.

1 Cook the chicken pieces according to your preference by steaming, roasting or boiling. When cooked, if using chicken breast fillets, cut the meat into thin strips and, if using thighs, shred the meat with your fingers. Put aside.

2 Boil or steam the prawns for 2–3 minutes, drain and refresh under cold running water then drain again. Put aside.

3 To make the spice paste, using a mortar and pestle, grind the shallots, garlic, chillies, galangal, turmeric, lemon grass and candlenuts together to form a paste.

4 Heat the oil in a heavy pan, stir in the spice paste and fry until fragrant. Add the *terasi* and palm sugar and stir for 3–4 minutes, until the paste begins to brown. Add the tomatoes, coriander, mint and lime juice and cook for 5–10 minutes, until the sauce is reduced and thick. Season to taste and turn into a large bowl. Leave to cool.

5 Add the chicken and prawns to the bowl and toss well together. Turn on to a serving dish and serve with the lime wedges to squeeze over and the chillies to chew on.

Serves four

500g/1¼lb chicken breast fillets or thighs

225g/8oz prawns (shrimp), shelled and deveined

30ml/2 tbsp groundnut (peanut) oil

5ml/1 tsp *terasi* (Indonesian shrimp paste)

10ml/2 tsp palm sugar

2 tomatoes, skinned, seeded and chopped

1 bunch fresh coriander (cilantro) leaves, chopped

1 bunch fresh mint leaves, chopped

juice of 1 lime

salt and ground black pepper

For the spice paste

2 shallots, chopped

2 garlic cloves, chopped

2–3 red chillies, seeded and chopped

25g/1oz galangal, chopped

15g/½oz fresh turmeric, chopped, or 2.5ml/½ tsp ground turmeric

1 lemon grass stalk, chopped

2 candlenuts, chopped

To serve

1 lime, quartered

2 green or red chillies, seeded and cut into quarters lengthways

Per Portion Energy 274kcal/1154kJ; Protein 41.6g; Carbohydrate 10.4g, of which sugars 8.7g; Fat 7.7g, of which saturates 1.1g; Cholesterol 197mg; Calcium 99mg; Fibre 2.2g; Sodium 193mg.

Serves four to six

30ml/2 tbsp coconut or groundnut (peanut) oil

6–8 garlic cloves, crushed whole

50g/2oz fresh root ginger, sliced into matchsticks

6 spring onions (scallions), cut into 2.5cm/1in pieces

5–10ml/1–2 tsp whole black peppercorns, crushed

30ml/2 tbsp palm or muscavado sugar

8–10 chicken thighs, or thighs and drumsticks

350g/12 oz pork tenderloin, cut into chunks

150ml/¼ pint/⅔ cup coconut or white wine vinegar

150ml/¼ pint/⅔ cup dark soy sauce

300ml/½ pint/1¼ cups chicken stock

2–3 bay leaves

salt

To serve

stir-fried greens

cooked rice

Cook's tip For the best flavour, make this dish the day before eating. Leave the cooked dish to cool, put in the refrigerator overnight, then reheat the next day.

Adobo chicken and pork cooked with vinegar and ginger
Adobo manok

Originally from Mexico, *adobo* has become the national dish of the Philippines. It can be made with chicken (*adobong manok*), with pork (*adobong baboy*) or with both, as in this recipe. It can also be prepared with fish, shellfish and vegetables, as the name *adobong* refers to the method – cooking in lots of vinegar, ginger and garlic – not the dish itself.

1 Heat the oil in a wok with a lid or a flameproof casserole, stir in the garlic and ginger and fry until they become fragrant and begin to colour. Add the spring onions and black pepper and stir in the sugar.

2 Add the chicken and pork to the wok or casserole and fry until they begin to colour. Pour in the vinegar, soy sauce and chicken stock and add the bay leaves. Bring to the boil, reduce the heat, cover and simmer gently for about 1 hour, until the meat is tender and the liquid has reduced.

3 Season the stew with salt to taste and serve with stir-fried greens and rice, over which the cooking liquid is spooned.

Per Portion Energy 270kcal/1135kJ; Protein 42.2g; Carbohydrate 9g, of which sugars 7.6g; Fat 7.4g, of which saturates 1.6g; Cholesterol 118mg; Calcium 24mg; Fibre 0.6g; Sodium 1892mg.

Sweet snacks and drinks

Sweet snacks and drinks

Along with most other culinary cultures of South-east Asia, the Indonesians prefer to eat fresh fruit at the end of a meal and sweet snacks throughout the day. This is because the meal is intended to be a balance of the five key flavour notes – salty, bitter, sour, spicy and sweet. The Filipinos, on the other hand, enjoy a sweet pudding at the end of a meal, as well as sweet snacks at any hour during the day.

For an island steeped in Hindu-Buddhist history, strewn with ancient temples and bubbling volcanoes, Java could evoke reams of poetic words, but there is only one word to describe the palate of its inhabitants and that is 'sweet'. The addictive, local palm sugar is used in both the savoury and sweet dishes of this region, more than any other part of Indonesia. Special sweet snacks include *kelepon*, green rice-flour dumplings filled with palm sugar, and *geplak*, sticky rice cakes made with palm sugar and coconut. The Filipinos share this sweet tooth, adding liberal amounts of palm sugar to their steamed rice cakes and sticky, fried bananas. The Filipinos have the added attraction of European-style, Spanish-influenced puddings, such as the ever-popular *leche flan* (Filipino Crème Caramel with Orange).

In spite of the Spanish influence, some native sweet dishes have survived, including *suman*, a sweet snack which can be made from rice, cassava or bananas, which are steamed in the hollow of a bamboo stem or wrapped in banana leaves, and served with fresh grated coconut and sugar. Another traditional Filipino sweet snack is *buko* (the name refers to the local sweet coconut), which must be made with the tender flesh of young coconuts, as the internal coconut water and flesh are combined together with sugar and then frozen until it resembles a refreshing and delicate sorbet.

In Indonesia, many of the traditional sweet snacks are made from glutinous rice, sweetened with sugar and flavoured with fragrant leaves, then steamed in tiny packages woven from palm fronds. The concept of ending a meal with something sweet is alien to the Indonesian culture, where sweet snacks are enjoyed at any time of the day. With the Spanish and American influence on the modern culinary customs, the Filipinos indulge in both; a sweet snack at any time of day and a pudding to end the meal.

Above, from left to right *Black sticky rice pudding* (bubuh injin); *palm leaf; sticky coconut crêpes* (dadar).

Fresh fruit, on the other hand, is usually eaten at the end of the meal in both countries. With such an abundance of tropical treats, the choice is never dull – watermelon, pomegranates, apples, pineapples, mangoes, jackfruit, star fruit (carambola), mangosteens, snakeskin fruit, rambutan, sapodilla, passion fruit, sweet bananas and guava. Generally, all these fruits are eaten fresh when ripe, but some are chosen when immature and firm to be chopped up for salads, such as *rujak*, a crunchy, fruity salad served with a spicy sauce.

The Indonesians enjoy many fruit drinks but, as the nation is predominantly Muslim, the homemade spirits and alcoholic beverages are consumed to a lesser degree. Among the many delectable and refreshing tropical fruit drinks and syrupy iced drinks is the delightfully refreshing *es ketimun*, made with shredded cucumber, sugar syrup and lots of ice.

However, tea and coffee are where Indonesia excels. Originally set up by the Dutch, the tea and coffee plantations enhance the already stunning landscape tapestry of rice paddies. The majority of Indonesia's tea produce is black tea, three quarters of which is exported, but there is plenty left to satisfy the tea-drinking nation. Generally, tea is served black with sugar. Other teas include green tea and ginger tea, which is a popular morning beverage, particularly for peasants before they head out to work in the fields.

Indonesia is also the third largest coffee producer in the world. Plantations are found in the highlands of Java and Bali and in central Sulawesi and Sumatra. To drink coffee Indonesian style, you need to think of it as a pick-me-up, rather than a pleasant after-dinner digestive. You can ask for milky coffee (*kopi susu*), which is served with sweetened condensed milk, or have black coffee (*kopi tubruk*), which is chewy, gritty and sweet.

On a daily basis, most Filipinos drink juices made from pressed fresh fruit, such as passion fruit juice and a refreshing *soursop* juice. Kalamansi limes are used to make a cordial and the special *buko* coconut is sought after for its juice. A popular cocoa drink (*cacao*) is made by pounding the cocoa bean and infusing it in boiling water, sweetened with sugar.

Black tea is generally drunk among the Chinese communities and served in Chinese restaurants. A ginger-infused tea is drunk to aid the digestion, apart from in the cool air of the hilly regions where it is drunk at breakfast early in the morning. Coffee is traditionally reserved for special occasions in the Philippines and is offered to guests as a form of hospitality. However, traditions are changing and the current trend among youngsters and students in the cities is the coffee house scene where they can enjoy good coffee and browse through books.

Many Filipinos enjoy fermented drinks, in particular the sweet coconut wine, *tuba*. Throughout the islands, buckets hang from the leaves of palm trees which have been cut to release the sap. As the sap collects, bubbles form and the liquid ferments into a wine that is believed to have aphrodisiacal qualities. Other fermented drinks include local wines made from rice, coconuts and bananas, and the powerful spirit, *lumbanog*, made from coconut, raisins and other fruit.

Above, from left to right *Fiesta coconut rice cake* (suman); *mango; fresh ginger tea* (bandrek).

Serves three to four

15ml/1 tbsp palm or coconut oil

15ml/2 tbsp coconut oil

5ml/1 tsp cardamom seeds

225g/8oz/1½ cups fresh coconut, finely grated or shredded

60ml/4 tbsp palm sugar

pinch of salt

sugar, to sprinkle (optional)

For the crêpes

115g/4oz/1 cup plus 30ml/2 tbsp rice flour

30ml/2 tbsp tapioca flour or cornflour (cornstarch)

2 eggs, beaten

about 400ml/14fl oz/1⅔ cups water

corn or vegetable oil, for frying

salt

Variation To ring the changes, you can add ginger to the filling and sprinkle the hot, sticky crêpes with icing (confectioners') sugar.

Sticky coconut crêpes
Dadar

A great favourite at street stalls, this is one of the Indonesian sweet snacks that tourists in Bali and Java rave about. Indonesians love them too, devouring them in great quantities, as they are so simple and tasty. Made with the same batter used for savoury spring rolls, the crêpes are filled with a sticky coconut mixture and served at room temperature, or fried in a pan and served hot.

1 To make the crêpes, sift the rice flour and tapioca or cornflour into a bowl and make a well in the centre. Add the beaten eggs and palm oil into the well and gradually pour in the water, whisking all the time, until a smooth batter is formed. Season the batter with salt and leave to rest for 30 minutes.

2 Heat a heavy, non-stick pancake or crêpe pan and, using a piece of kitchen paper, wipe a little of the oil all over the surface. Using a small cup or ladle, add a little of batter to the pan, tilting it at the same time to spread the batter evenly over the base. In total there should be enough batter to make 12 crêpes. Reduce the heat and cook the pancakes gently until the batter sets and lifts at the edges, then flip the crêpe over and cook on the other side until just lightly browned. Carefully lift the crêpe on to a plate and repeat with the remaining batter.

3 In a heavy, non-stick pan, heat the palm or coconut oil and stir in the cardamom seeds. Toss in the shredded coconut, and then add the sugar and salt. Over a low heat, toss the coconut continuously for 3–5 minutes, until it caramelizes. Remove from the heat and leave to cool.

4 Place a crêpe on a flat surface in front of you and heap 15–30ml/1–2 tbsp of caramelized coconut just off centre. Fold the edge nearest to you over the filling, tuck in the sides, and roll over to form a log. Repeat with the remaining crêpes and filling.

5 Serve the crêpe at room temperature, or heat in a lightly oiled, heavy frying pan with an extra sprinkling of sugar to make them sticky, and serve hot.

Per Portion Energy 475kcal/1972kJ; Protein 7g; Carbohydrate 38.6g, of which sugars 1.6g; Fat 32.4g, of which saturates 17.8g; Cholesterol 95mg; Calcium 30mg; Fibre 4.2g; Sodium 48mg.

Filipino flambéed banana fritters
Maruya

You can find deep-fried banana fritters at food stalls and cafés in Vietnam, Thailand, Malaysia, Singapore, Indonesia and the Philippines. The only variation is the type of banana that is used, as there are so many in South-east Asia. In Indonesia the deep-fried fritters are called *pisang goreng* and in the Philippines they are known as *maruya*. This Filipino recipe is particularly delicious as grated ginger and coconut are added to the batter. Local rum is used to the flambé the bananas, which are then served with coconut cream.

1 First make the batter. Sift the flour, baking powder and salt into a large bowl. Make a well in the centre and drop in the beaten eggs. Gradually pour in the coconut milk, beating all the time with a whisk or wooden spoon, until the batter is smooth. Beat in the sugar, grated ginger and coconut. Leave the batter to stand for 30 minutes.

2 Cut the banana in half and cut each half lengthways. Beat the batter again and drop in the bananas, making sure they are well coated.

3 Heat enough oil for deep-frying in a wok or deep pan. Working in batches and using a pair of tongs, lift 2–3 bananas out of the batter and lower them into the oil.

4 Fry the bananas until crisp and golden brown, then lift them out and drain on kitchen paper. Dust with icing or caster sugar and eat warm with your fingers.

5 Alternatively, to flambé the banana fritters, arrange the deep-fried bananas in a wide, heavy pan and place over a medium heat. Sprinkle the sugar over the top and toss the bananas in the pan until they are sticky and slightly caramelized. Lower the heat, pour in the rum and set alight. (Have a lid handy to smother the flames if necessary.) Spoon the rum over the bananas until caramelized and serve immediately with coconut cream.

Serves three to four

6–8 small or 3 large ripe bananas

corn or vegetable oil, for deep-frying

icing (confectioners') sugar or caster (superfine) sugar, for dusting

coconut cream, to serve

For the batter

115g/4oz/1 cup plain (all-purpose) flour

5ml/1 tsp baking powder

pinch of salt

2 eggs, lightly beaten

400g/14oz can coconut milk

15ml/1 tbsp palm sugar

25g/1oz fresh root ginger, finely grated

50g/2oz fresh coconut, grated, or desiccated (dry unsweetened shredded) coconut

To flambé

15–30ml/1–2 tbsp sugar

rice alcohol or rum

coconut cream

Per Portion Energy 407kcal/1710kJ; Protein 7.8g; Carbohydrate 53.3g, of which sugars 29.7g; Fat 19.7g, of which saturates 8.8g; Cholesterol 95mg; Calcium 95mg; Fibre 3.4g; Sodium 151mg.

Sweet spring rolls with banana and jackfruit
Turones de saba

"*Turon turon*" cry the Filipino street vendors as you walk by, luring you to try their delicious sweet spring rolls, which can be sprinkled with sugar and eaten with the fingers, or served as a pudding with a caramel sauce. Traditionally, the Filipinos use a short fat banana called *saba* and jackfruit (*nangka*), which is one of the largest fruits in the world, smooth in texture with a lovely sweet aroma. For this recipe use ordinary bananas and, if you cannot find fresh jackfruit in South-east Asian food shops, substitute it with pineapple.

Serves four to six

12 spring roll wrappers or *lumpia* wrappers

2 firm, ripe bananas, thinly sliced diagonally

175g/6oz jackfruit, thinly sliced

30–45ml/2–3 tbsp palm or muscovado (molasses) sugar

1–2 eggs, beaten

corn or vegetable oil, for deep-frying

For the caramel sauce

115g/4oz/1 cup sugar

120ml/4fl oz/½ cup water

250ml/8fl oz/1 cup unsweetened coconut milk or coconut cream

Cook's tip Filipinos have a very sweet tooth and a love of condensed milk. This is very often used instead of a sweet sauce in puddings such as *turones de saba*, as it is quick and easy to prepare. Even if this caramel sauce is made, it may be further sweetened with a tablespoon or two of condensed milk.

1 First make the sauce. Put the sugar and water into a heavy pan and, shaking the pan occasionally, heat until it caramelizes. When the mixture starts to turn a rich brown, remove from the heat and stir in the coconut milk or coconut cream. Return the pan to the heat and continue stirring until the sauce thickens slightly. Remove from the heat and leave the sauce to rest.

2 Place a spring roll wrapper on a flat surface in front of you. Arrange, overlapping, 2–3 slices of banana with 2–3 slices of jackfruit 2.5cm/1in from the edge nearest to you. Sprinkle a little sugar over the fruit, then roll the nearest edge over the fruit, tuck in the ends and continue rolling into a loose log. (If it is too tight the wrapper will split open when fried.) Moisten the far edge with a little beaten egg to seal the roll so that the filling does not escape during the frying. Repeat with the remaining spring roll wrappers.

3 Heat enough oil in a wok or pan for deep frying. Working in batches, deep-fry the spring rolls for 3–4 minutes, until golden brown all over. Using tongs, lift the spring rolls out of the oil and drain on kitchen paper.

4 Quickly reheat the sauce. Arrange the spring rolls on a serving dish, or in individual bowls, and serve with the caramel sauce drizzled over the top.

Per Portion Energy 246kcal/1043kJ; Protein 4g; Carbohydrate 47.3g, of which sugars 37.1g; Fat 5.9g, of which saturates 1.1g; Cholesterol 63mg; Calcium 55mg; Fibre 1.2g; Sodium 72mg.

Indonesian black sticky rice pudding
Bubuh injin

Often called "forbidden rice", black sticky rice is usually flavoured with pandanus leaves but you can use a vanilla pod or ginger instead.

1 Put the rice in a large bowl, cover generously with cold water and leave to soak for 4 hours. Rinse the rice under cold running water and drain.

2 Put the rice in a pan, cover with 300ml/½ pint/1¼ cups water and bring it to the boil. Stir in 45ml/3 tbsp of the sugar until dissolved, and then add the pandanus leaves, vanilla pod or ginger. Reduce the heat and simmer for 10–15 minutes, until the water has been absorbed. Remove from the heat, cover and leave to steam for 10 minutes.

3 Meanwhile, pour the coconut milk into a separate pan and bring to the boil. Stir in the remaining sugar and the salt until the sugar has dissolved. Keep warm.

4 In small, heavy frying pan, quickly dry-fry the coconut, tossing it all the time, until it gives off a lovely aroma and turns golden brown. Turn it into a bowl.

5 Remove the pandanus leaves, vanilla pod of ginger from the rice and spoon the into individual serving bowls. Drizzle the hot coconut milk over the top and sprinkle with the coconut.

Serves four to six

225g/8oz/1 cup plus 30ml/2 tbsp black sticky rice

60–75ml/4–5 tbsp palm sugar

2–3 pandanus (screwpine) leaves, 1 vanilla pod or 25g/1oz fresh root ginger

400g/14oz can coconut milk

a pinch of salt

60ml/4 tbsp desiccated (dry unsweetened shredded) coconut

Cook's tip Black sticky rice is available in South-east Asian stores. It is often sold as Indonesian black rice.

Per Portion Energy 249kcal/1044kJ; Protein 4g; Carbohydrate 42.5g, of which sugars 14.4g; Fat 7g, of which saturates 5.5g; Cholesterol 0mg; Calcium 33mg; Fibre 1.4g; Sodium 78mg.

Fiesta coconut rice cake
Suman

The small quantity of spring onions included in the recipe give the rice cakes an interesting taste, which is much enjoyed by Filipinos. The rice cakes can be steamed in banana or palm leaves, or cooked in a heavy, non-stick pan, as in this recipe, then cut into wedges and served on coconut palm leaves.

1 Put the rice in a sieve (strainer), rinse under cold running water until the water runs clear then drain. Put the rice and the coconut milk in a heavy, non-stick, shallow pan and bring to the boil, stirring to prevent the rice sticking to the bottom. Reduce the heat and simmer for 10 minutes, until the rice sticks to the back of a wooden spoon.

2 Add the sugar to the rice and stir until it dissolves. Add the ginger, spring onion, vanilla essence and lime juice. Simmer until all the liquid has been absorbed. Remove from the heat, cover and leave to steam and cool.

3 Meanwhile, put the coconut in a small, heavy frying pan and dry-fry until it turns golden brown and gives off a nutty aroma.

4 When the rice has cooled and is fairly solid, cut it into a criss-cross pattern and lift out the diamond-shaped wedges with a spatula. Place on individual squares of banana or coconut palm leaf. Sprinkle a little of the coconut over the top and serve with lime wedges to squeeze over the cakes.

Serves four to six

225g/8oz/1 cup plus 30ml/2 tbsp sticky rice

600ml/1 pint/2½ cups coconut milk

225g/8oz/1 cup palm or muscavado (molasses) sugar

25g/1oz fresh root ginger, finely grated

1 spring onion (scallion), white parts only, very finely chopped

2–3 drops vanilla essence (extract)

juice of 2 kalamansi or ordinary limes

To serve

banana or palm leaves

30–45ml/2–3 tbsp desiccated (dry unsweetened shredded) coconut

1 lime, cut into wedges

Per Portion Energy 323kcal/1365kJ; Protein 4.1g; Carbohydrate 76g, of which sugars 44.1g; Fat 1g, of which saturates 0.2g; Cholesterol 0mg; Calcium 56mg; Fibre 0g; Sodium 114mg.

Filipino crème caramel with orange
Leche flan

A legacy of the Spanish, this is a very popular sweet snack in the Philippines. It varies marginally from a classic, light crème caramel to a heavier, flatter version made with condensed milk and evaporated milk. Both are delicious but the Filipino preference is for the heavier, Spanish-influenced version.

1 Preheat the oven to 160°C/325°F/Gas 3. Put a round 20cm/8in ovenproof dish or individual 5cm/2in dishes into the oven to warm.

2 To make the caramel, put the sugar and orange juice into a heavy pan and, over a high heat, stir until the sugar has dissolved. Bring the mixture to the boil and leave to bubble, resisting the temptation to stir, until dark golden in colour.

3 Remove the dishes or dishes from the oven and pour in the caramel, swirling it around so that it coats the bottom and the sides. Put aside to let the caramel harden.

4 Meanwhile, put the evaporated milk, condensed milk, orange rind or vanilla essence into a pan and heat until scalding but not boiling. Remove from the heat, cover and leave the milk to infuse for 15–20 minutes.

Serves four

2 x 400g/14oz cans evaporated milk

150g/5½oz can condensed milk

grated rind of 1 orange or a few drops of vanilla essence (extract)

4 eggs

2 egg yolks

For the caramel

150g/5oz caster (superfine) sugar

75ml/5 tbsp fresh orange juice, strained

5 In a large bowl, lightly whisk the eggs and egg yolks together. Reheat the milk then strain into the egg mixture, whisking all the time. Strain into the dish or dishes.

6 Place the dish or dishes in a roasting tin and pour in boiling water until it comes halfway up the sides of the dish or dishes. Carefully transfer the roasting tin to the oven and cook for about 1 hour, until the crème caramel is set. (It should be firm to the touch but with a hint of wobble as it will continue to cook a little when removed from the oven.) Leave to cool then chill in the refrigerator overnight.

7 To serve, press the edges lightly to release it from the dish, and then use a sharp, thin knife to ease it away. Place a plate over the top of the dish and invert it, giving it a gentle shake. Remove the dish and serve.

Cook's tip If you like, you can decorate the crème caramel with threads of syrupy orange rind. Using a zester, shred the rind into fine threads and simmer in a syrup of sugar and water (made with 30ml/2 tbsp sugar to 30ml/2 tbsp water) until they look smooth and shiny. Using a slotted spoon, remove from the syrup and scatter over the top of the pudding.

Per Portion Energy 398kcal/1678kJ; Protein 17.9g; Carbohydrate 54.8g, of which sugars 54.8g; Fat 13.5g, of which saturates 6.5g; Cholesterol 226mg; Calcium 461mg; Fibre 0g; Sodium 241mg.

Spice island ice cream
Maluku ice cream

With such a range of tropical fruit and spices, there is almost no limit to the flavours of Indonesian ice cream. In this delicious ice cream, warming spices, which reflect the region's history of Indian and Arab traders, are combined with the Indonesian passion for something cool and sweet.

1 In a heavy pan, heat the cream with the spices until scalding. Remove the pan from the heat and leave the cream to infuse until cool.

2 In a separate pan, heat the sugar and water together, stirring all the time, until the sugar has dissolved. Bring to the boil and boil for 2–3 minutes, then lower the heat and simmer for 5 minutes. Remove from the eat and leave to infuse for 10 minutes.

3 Whisk the eggs together in a bowl. Gradually, trickle in the hot syrup, whisking all the time, until the mixture becomes light and airy like a mousse. Strain the spice-infused cream into the mixture and whisk well together until thoroughly blended.

4 Pour the mixture into an ice cream maker and churn until frozen, according to the manufacturer's instructions. Alternatively, pour into a freezer container and freeze, uncovered, for 1–2 hours until beginning to set around the edges. Turn into a bowl and, beat to break up the ice crystals. Return to the freezer container and repeat the beating again, then cover and freeze until firm. Serve with a sprinkling of cinnamon or nutmeg.

Serves six

500ml/17fl oz/generous 2 cups double (heavy) cream

6–8 cloves

6–8 cardamom seeds

3–4 star anise

3 cinnamon sticks

90g/3½oz/½ cup caster (superfine) sugar

150ml/¼ pint/⅔ cup water

4 large eggs

ground cinnamon or nutmeg, to sprinkle

Per Portion Energy 522kcal/2157kJ; Protein 5.6g; Carbohydrate 17.1g, of which sugars 17.1g; Fat 48.5g, of which saturates 28.9g; Cholesterol 241mg; Calcium 68mg; Fibre 0g; Sodium 66mg.

Filipino mango ice cream
Manila managa ice cream

Two of the most popular ice creams in the Philippines are made from fresh mangoes and coconuts. Ice creams are sometimes served as puddings in restaurants and at special feasts, otherwise they are enjoyed at any time of the day and in the evening at ice cream parlours and street stalls.

1 In a bowl, whisk the egg yolks and sugar together until light and frothy. In a heavy pan, heat the milk until scalding and then slowly pour the milk into the egg mixture, whisking all the time. Strain the milk and egg mixture back into the rinsed pan. Heat, stirring all the time, until thickened but do not allow the mixture to boil. Leave to cool.

2 Mash the mango with a fork, or purée it in an electric blender or food processor.

3 Strain the cooled custard into a large bowl. Add the cream and whisk together. Beat in the mango purée until well mixed.

4 Pour the mixture into an ice cream maker and churn until frozen, according to the manufacturer's instructions. Alternatively, pour into a freezer container and freeze, uncovered, for 1–2 hours until beginning to set around the edges. Turn into a bowl and beat to break up the ice crystals. Return to the freezer container and repeat the beating again, then cover and freeze until firm.

Serves four to six

6 egg yolks

115g/4oz/heaped ½ cup caster (superfine) sugar

500ml/17fl oz/2¼ cups full fat (whole) or skimmed milk

350g/12oz mango flesh (about 3 mangoes)

300ml/½ pint/1¼ cups double (heavy) cream

Cook's tip Serve the ice cream with thin slices of fresh mango to emphasize the flavours of this tropical treat.

Per Portion Energy 466kcal/1941kJ; Protein 7.2g; Carbohydrate 35.4g, of which sugars 35.2g; Fat 33.9g, of which saturates 19.2g; Cholesterol 275mg; Calcium 167mg; Fibre 2g; Sodium 59mg.

Fresh ginger tea
Bandrek

Ginger tea is a speciality of the high-altitude regions of Indonesia, such as Dieng Plateau and the hill trails of Bandung. Often you will find an old woman making the tea in the small hill shelters made of bamboo, where people stop to rest and drink a glass of this refreshing and stimulating brew. Ginger tea is also the preferred breakfast beverage in the Philippines as it is regarded as warming and stimulates the digestion. The traditional Filipino method of making the tea is to wrap the fresh ginger in a piece of muslin and then squeeze out the juices.

1 Put the water, ginger, cinnamon sticks, peppercorns and sugar into a pan and bring to the boil, stirring until the sugar has dissolved. Boil vigorously for 2 minutes, then reduce the heat and simmer for at least 15 minutes.

2 Divide the shredded coconut between four heatproof glasses and strain over the hot ginger tea. Serve immediately, with a spoon to scoop up the coconut.

Serves four

1 litre/1¾ pints/4 cups water

40g/1½oz fresh root ginger, sliced

1–2 cinnamon sticks

5ml/1 tsp black peppercorns

30ml/2 tbsp palm sugar

115g/4oz/¾ cup coconut flesh, finely shredded

Cook's tip The tea improves with standing so, if convenient, you can make it in advance and reheat it before serving.

Per Portion Energy 120kcal/500kJ; Protein 0.9g; Carbohydrate 8.8g, of which sugars 8.8g; Fat 9.3g, of which saturates 8g; Cholesterol 0mg; Calcium 8mg; Fibre 2.1g; Sodium 5mg.

Serves two

30ml/2 tbsp preserved sweet beans

30ml/2 tbsp preserved sugar-palm fruit

30ml/2 tbsp preserved purple yam

30ml/2 tbsp preserved
macapuno coconut

crushed ice

30ml/2 tbsp condensed milk

2 lychee, stoned (pitted)

2 half moon slices ripe mango, with
their skin, to decorate

Iced preserved fruit and legume drink
Halo-halo

Literally translated as "mixed-mixed", this is the Filipino version of Vietnam's famous rainbow drink. Packed with fruit preserves and chilled with crushed ice, over which sweet condensed milk is poured, this drink is popular with children, young people in cafés and working men. Known as a "working man's drink", it is really more of a snack and is well worth sampling on a hot day.

1 Divide the preserved ingredients between two tall glasses, layering them in any order you want. Fill the rest of the glass with crushed ice to 2.5cm/1⁄2in from the top. Spoon the condensed milk over the ice so that it runs down the inside of the glass.

2 Place a lychee on top of each drink. Make a small incision in the middle of each mango slice and use to decorate the glasses by securing them on the edge of the glass rim. Serve immediately, with a long-handled spoon to reach down into the depths of the preserves.

Cook's tip All the preserved ingredients needed to make *halo-halo* are available in jars in Chinese and South east Asian food stores.

Per Portion Energy 182kcal/775kJ; Protein 4.2g; Carbohydrate 39.4g, of which sugars 39.3g; Fat 2g, of which saturates 1g; Cholesterol 5mg; Calcium 94mg; Fibre 5.2g; Sodium 31mg.

Filipino mango and lime drink
Manga at kalalmansi inomin

The tropical islands of the Philippines are home to a wide variety of different mangoes, some of which you do not see anywhere else. Most of these fruits are varieties for eating, as opposed to cooking, and when ripe they are juicy and buttery, melting in the mouth with an exquisite tropical flavour. As there is such an abundance of ripe mangoes readily available, many are used to make either mango ice cream or this drink, which is often enjoyed at breakfast or as a refreshing snack in the heat of the day.

1 Put the mango flesh in a blender or food processor and whiz to form a purée. Sweeten with sugar according to your taste. Divide the purée between two tall glasses.

2 Spoon a layer of crushed ice over the top of the mango purée then pour over the lime juice. Make a small incision in each slice of lime and use to decorate the glasses by wedging them on the edge of the glass rim.

3 Serve immediately, with a long spoon or a straw.

Serves two

4 very ripe mangoes, stoned (pitted)

15–30ml/1–2 tbsp sugar

crushed ice

juice of 1–2 kalamansi or ordinary limes

2 slices fresh lime, to decorate

Cook's tip The sweet-toothed Filipinos sometimes purée the mangoes with condensed milk, or pour the milk over the ice on top of the mango.

Per Portion Energy 230kcal/987kJ; Protein 2.2g; Carbohydrate 58g, of which sugars 57.1g; Fat 0.6g, of which saturates 0.3g; Cholesterol 0mg; Calcium 44mg; Fibre 7.8g; Sodium 7mg.

Avocado juice
Jus apokat

One of many unusual sweet delights found at street stalls in Indonesia and the Philippines, this thick, syrupy avocado juice falls somewhere between a snack and a drink. Once again, the South-east Asian passion for condensed milk gives this drink its finishing touch.

1 Put the sugar and water in a heavy pan and heat gently, stirring all the time, until the sugar has dissolved. Bring to the boil then remove from the heat and leave to cool.

2 When the sugar syrup is cold, put the flesh of the avocados in a large bowl or food processor, add the cooled sugar syrup and mash or blend together until smooth.

3 Put the ice cubes or crushed ice into two tall glasses, spoon in the avocado mixture then drizzle the condensed milk over the top. Serve immediately, with a long spoon so that the drinkers can mix the avocado with the condensed milk at their leisure.

Serves two

30ml/2 tbsp sugar

30ml/2 tbsp water

2 ripe avocados

a handful of ice cubes or crushed ice

45–60ml/2 tbsp condensed milk

Per Portion 324kcal/1353kJ; Protein 3.9g; Carbohydrate 30.1g, of which sugars 28.7g; Fat 21.6g, of which saturates 5.5g; Cholesterol 8mg; Calcium 84mg; Fibre 3.4g; Sodium 39mg.

Index

GHILLIE BAŞAN'S ACKNOWLEDGEMENTS

First, I would like to thank Vilma and her husband, Romy, for all their help with the Filipino recipes and the research – the best part of which has been eating all the food! In Malaysia, Singapore, and Indonesia, I would like to thank Ravinder Singh, Joseph Toyo, Peter Grant, and Dance Malangki in Menado – all expert guides on the ground. My children, Yasmin and Zeki, also deserve a mention as they have had to learn to cope with the long hours I work.

Once again the *Essentials of Asian Cuisine* by Corinne Trang proved invaluable, the Lonely Planet *World Food Indonesia* was a useful and informative guide, and *Culture and History* by Nick Joaquin provided some interesting facts on the Philippines. At Anness, I would like to thank Emma Clegg and Lucy Doncaster for all their help and I am very fortunate to be able to thank Martin Brigdale again for his superb photography – he has given life to my words in several books.

VILMA LAUS' ACKNOWLEDGEMENTS

I would like to express my profound gratitude to the late Clarisse Dayson and to the late Sir and Lady Maxwell Joseph, who helped me to fulfil my dreams. I would also like to thank all my friends in Aberdeenshire, especially Mr and Mrs Holroyd and Dr and Mrs Fulton, for all their help and kindness. And, I would like to mention my husband Romy, who has helped with this book and shares my passion for spreading the word about Filipino food!

PUBLISHER'S ACKNOWLEDGEMENTS

Publisher: **Joanna Lorenz**
Senior Managing Editor: **Conor Kilgallon**
Project Editors: **Lucy Doncaster** and **Emma Clegg**
Copy Editor: **Susanna Tee**
Home Economist: **Lucy McKelvie**
Stylist: **Helen Trent**
Designer: **Lisa Tai**
Production Controller: **Wendy Lawson**

© Anness Publishing Ltd 2007

Front cover shows Fresh Spring Rolls with Palm Heart – for recipe, see page 80

The publisher would like to thank the following for the use of their pictures in the book (l=left, r=right, t=top, b=bottom). **Alamy:** 8; 9; 10; 12b; 15t; 17b; 18; 19t; 23b. **Corbis:** 13t; 19b; 20; 21; 22tr. **Susan Doncaster:** 7b; 12t; 14b. **Rob Highton:** 6b; 7b. **Travel Ink Photo Library:** 11; 17t.